A Parish in Perspec

Dr Geoff Taylor has lived in South Hackney for over thirty years and has been involved in a wide variety of community activities, many of which have involved the church of St John of Jerusalem. For the last fifteen years, he has regularly played the organ for Sunday services, and he chairs the trustees of both South Hackney Parochial Charities and St John Hackney Joint Estates Charities. In May 2002, he was elected a Member of Hackney Borough Council for the Victoria ward, an area broadly coincident with the parish of South Hackney. In the guise of the first Rector, he occasionally leads walks around the parish as it was in the 1840s.

A Parish in Perspective

*A History of
the Church and Parish
of St John of Jerusalem
South Hackney*

Geoff Taylor

Published by
the Rector and Churchwardens
of St John of Jerusalem with Christ Church
South Hackney
London E9

2002

Copyright © Geoffrey Noel Taylor 2002

Published in England in 2002
by the Rector and Churchwardens of
St John of Jerusalem with Christ Church
South Hackney, London E9

The right of Geoffrey Noel Taylor to be identified
as the author of the work has been asserted by him in
accordance with the Copyright, Designs and Patents Act 1988.

*The financial support of
Lord Amherst of Hackney and June Pipe
for this publication is gratefully acknowledged.*

All rights reserved

ISBN 0-9544019-0-5

Typeset by Regent Typesetting, London

Printed by The Cromwell Press, Trowbridge, Wiltshire

Cover photo:
War memorial and tower, St John of Jerusalem Church
by Geoff Taylor

I married Elizabeth Hunter in St John of Jerusalem Church in 1974.
During more than a quarter of a century we have taken part together
in a wide range of activities in and around this building.
This book is dedicated to her.

Contents

Acknowledgements   ix
Author's Note   x
List of Illustrations   xi
List of Plates   xiii

Introduction – A Building Poses Some Questions   1

Chapter I   1800 to 1850: From Hamlet to Fully-fledged Parish   3

Chapter II   1851 to Around 1900: A Flourishing Victorian Parish   47

Chapter III   Around 1900 to the 1970s: Lean Years   97

Chapter IV   Since the 1970s: South Hackney Revitalised   131

Envoi   A Shade Returns   157

The following articles will be found scattered through the Chapters:

The Order of St John of Jerusalem   6

South Hackney's Rector Plays a National Role:
The Rev Henry Handley Norris MA   12

Architectural Theorist and Church Architect:
Edward Charles Hakewill FRIBA   26

The *Illustrated London News* shows its readers round the New Church   34

The First Rector Leaves the Stage   44

Lessons from the Graveyard   58

To See Ourselves as Others See Us: Walter Southgate	61
South Hackney Musician Finds a Wider Public: John E West FRCO FRAM	72
Differences of Approach	82
A Poet in the Parish: The Rev Walter John Ferrar MA	90
The Ringing of the Bells	99
Responses to War: Rehabilitation and Reconstruction	105
Arthur 'Virge' Erridge MGPS, Stained Glass Artist	112
South Hackney's Wonderful Windows	117
An Unexpected Career: The Rev Prebendary Patricia Ann Farquhar	138
Who Goes There?	144
What Future for South Hackney Church?	152
Appendix 1 *The Rectors of South Hackney*	161
Appendix 2 *The Vicars of Christ Church, Gore Road*	162
Appendix 3 *£sd – Money before Decimals*	162
Principal Sources	163
Notes	167
Index	171

Acknowledgements

I knew many of the characters who appear in the latter part of this history, and I have often kicked myself for not having quizzed some of them while they were alive about the history of the church to whose community I have belonged for over thirty years; I am grateful to several of them for not having waited to be asked for stories of the past. I am also grateful to the many present and past members of the congregation, clergy and others whom I have been able to interview, for their willingness to share memories and views with me.

I have also been helped by representatives of families whose members have played a part in the history of the church, especially the fourth Baron Amherst of Hackney, Francis Erridge, Bob Hakewill and Hugh Norris. Andrew Houston brought John E West to my attention. Dr Melvyn Brooks of Tel Shalom, Karkur, Israel has generously given me help from his archive of Hackney history. Wendy King of the London Diocesan Board for Schools provided information about the parish school.

I am grateful to those who have given me authority to use illustrations; they are acknowledged individually in the captions. I am particularly grateful to Christine Boyd who took some photographs especially for this book. Crown copyright material held in the National Monuments Record is reproduced by permission of English Heritage acting under licence from the Controller of HM Stationery Office.

Once again I wish to express my gratitude to Lord Amherst and June Pipe for the financial support that has made this publication possible.

Author's Note

It has been a pleasure to write this history of the church and parish of St John of Jerusalem with Christ Church, South Hackney. I am grateful to the Patron and the Rector for the invitation to do so. It is not however an official book; I alone am responsible for the opinions and judgements expressed here.

I hesitate to let the book go to the printer, for over the last few years and often quite unprompted, people have turned up with new and interesting information about South Hackney. There will no doubt be more; but then, there will always be more. I am hoping that readers will be prompted to bring further information or archival material – as well as corrections – to my attention. Visitors to the church's website (www.sjoj.org.uk) are asked to sign the visitors book; it is a wonderful opportunity for you to add your memories and reflections to the record. Second editions of books like this would be better than the first, benefiting as they would from the help of readers; it is an unfortunate fact of life that books like this don't have second editions!

I have a niggling feeling that there is some connection between the dedication of the church to St John of Jerusalem, the author of *The Temple* and the Freemasons. I have been unable to demonstrate any such link; perhaps a reader will be able either to do so or to show that I am following a false scent here.

When I came to live in South Hackney thirty years ago, I was welcomed into this community and encouraged to make it my own. I hope that this book will perhaps help others (in Dr Spooner's lovely phrase) to enter into the inheritance of this place.

Geoff Taylor
South Hackney, October 2002

List of Illustrations

The Prior's House, Well Street hamlet — 5
Copyright: Hackney Archives Department

The heart of the new parish of South Hackney, 1831 — 10–11
Copyright: Hackney Archives Department

The Norris family mansion, about 1840 — 13
Copyright: Hackney Archives Department

Part of the original Monger's Almshouses, built in 1669 — 20
Copyright: Hackney Archives Department

A parish beadle, 1829 — 23

The proposed church of St John of Jerusalem, South Hackney, 1845 — 30

The interior of the church in the 1860s — 33
Crown copyright: NMR

The second building to house the parochial school, 1847
Copyright: London Metropolitan Archives — 38

The Monger Almshouse as rebuilt in 1847 — 41

South Hackney parish's Address to the Queen against Popish Aggression, 1850 — 43
Copyright: London Metropolitan Archives

The original Norris Almshouse of 1852 — 49
Copyright: Hackney Archives Department

The interior of St John of Jerusalem church, 1851 — 51

The interior of Christ Church, Gore Road, about 1920 — 53
Crown copyright: NMR

The chancel of St John of Jerusalem church in the 1880s — 55
Copyright: London Metropolitan Archives

St John of Jerusalem church from King Edward's Road in about 1905 — 57

Poster advertising Lent services at St John of Jerusalem church, 1853	65
Copyright: London Metropolitan Archives	
Queen's College – a long metre hymn tune by John E West	69
John E West FRCO FRAM	74
The first Rectory, about 1873	81
Copyright: Hackney Archives Department	
The tower and soaring spire proposed for Christ Church, Gore Road	95
The War Memorial	102
The view from the pew in the 1930s	103
Arthur Erridge	113
Donald Potter's low-relief of 'Christ and the Children'	121
The new Norris House, 1969	124
The interior of St John of Jerusalem church in the mid-1960s	127
Poster for the autumn bazaar, 1972	133
The Reverend Prebendary Patricia Farquhar	139
The Bishop of Stepney re-opens Monger House, 1997	148
The reordering at the west end proposed by Mark Julian in 2002	154
The interior of St John of Jerusalem church in about 1985	158

List of Plates

Plate 1 The first St John of Jerusalem Church in South Hackney, built in 1810
Copyright: Hackney Archives Department

Plate 2 The Rev Henry Handley Norris MA by Thomas Phillips RA
Copyright: Christine Boyd

Plate 3 The memorial tablet to Mother Alice Bannister
Copyright: Christine Boyd

Plate 4 The new south transept window by Arthur Erridge, 1955

Plate 5 Window in memory of Dorothy and Arthur Baker
Copyright: Christine Boyd

Introduction

A Building Poses Some Questions

On a large traffic island in Hackney, a mile or so north-east of Liverpool Street station and at the heart of the variegated community which estate agents like to call Victoria Park Village, stands a Victorian gothic church, its position signalled from afar by its bright green copper spire. Despite a brief appearance in detective literature in Barbara Vine's *Asta's Book*, it's not a particularly famous church. Its claim to what fame it has is that it is one of the biggest parish churches in London, built by a leading figure in the early nineteenth century Church of England. But by and large its history is the history of ordinary churchgoing Londoners and the way they have been affected by and responded to religious, social and political developments over the last two centuries.

    The building silently prompts the visitor to ask questions about it. How did it come to be named after a saint who appears in no dictionary of saints? What is the meaning of that bizarrely inappropriate spire? Why was the church made so large? What purpose is served by an aisle over four metres wide? Are the odd pillars and short bays at the west end a mistake? Why is the tracery of the north transept window different from that of the south? How is it that a church with a finely vaulted apse and well-made timber roofs on nave and transepts suffers the indignity of a crossing covered by painted planks? Why is the chancel so sparsely furnished? How did the church come to have such excellent twentieth century stained glass? Why are the slates on opposite sides of the roof different in colour? Whose is the portrait in the south transept?

    Interesting as it is in itself, what brings this – or any – building to life are the activities that it has housed and the ideas that informed them. Unlike a building, the traces of such activities and ideas are easily lost. When people weed out old papers, they often keep the dry documents and destroy the ones that in their various ways answer the most interesting questions about life-gone-by. How has the position of women in this place changed over the last two centuries? In what ways have people's religious attitudes and practices changed? What part has this church played in the wider social life of the area? How has demographic change affected this community? What was it like to live hereabouts in time gone by? How did people in the past get things done? What sorts of people were responsible for the buildings we take for granted?

These are some of the many questions that this book answers. It provides a straightforward account of the history of South Hackney parish, church, and church life, setting it in the wider historical perspective. Scattered through the chapters of history will be found a series of articles, identified by their appearance in boxes. They bring to life some of the figures connected with the church in South Hackney and deal with a variety of topics that illuminate the church's history.

Chapter I

1800 to 1850: From Hamlet to Fully-Fledged Parish

South Hackney in a Changing World

South Hackney began the nineteenth century as a collection of small rural hamlets in the ancient parish of Hackney; by the middle of the century, it was a parish in its own right and beginning to be developed as a suburb; by 1900, it was a heavily built-up part of London. This visible, local change was symptomatic of the astonishing and rapid changes England was experiencing in these years, changes that were hard for people to cope with, challenging traditional ideas and transforming lives in every part of society.

For a start, the population of the London area rocketed from one million in 1801 to seven million in 1901 as nutrition and health improved and people moved in from the countryside. Much of the increased urban population began to live further and further out from the old City of London, engulfing old villages such as Hackney. This was made possible by improvements in transport, especially the coming of the railways in the 1840s, which not only enabled people to commute to work in the City but also allowed food to be brought from further away than the market gardens of nearby places like Hackney.

Then there were sweeping political and social changes. Until 1815, Britain was fighting the first industrialised war, against a France which was exporting its Revolutionary ideas across continental Europe. Despite a natural conservative backlash, these ideas and the changes in the economy caused by industrialisation meant that a decisive move towards real democratisation could not be delayed after 1832. Those same industrial and economic changes demanded more of the workforce. Although there was still work for unskilled labourers, some elementary or vocational education was increasingly needed to obtain a job. Yet for decades the provision of this education was not seen as the business of government; it was left to local initiative, along with health, the support of the poor and even road building.

In religion too changes were afoot. The Church of England was broadly identified with the authorities – monarchy, government, aristocracy, magistracy – so anyone who wanted political change almost inevitably abandoned the established church. In any case, people were already doing that for other reasons: apart from the impact of new ideas on their traditional religious beliefs, people who moved to urban areas from the countryside felt less social pressure to attend church. If the less well-off belonged to any religious body, it was usually to one of the non-conformist groups which had developed during the eighteenth century, when much of the Church of England had lost its spiritual vigour, leaving serious evangelism and the popular consideration of religious matters to such groups as the Methodists and Unitarians.

The Church of England in Hackney in the Early Nineteenth Century

In 1800, the parish of Hackney still stretched from Grove Street hamlet – the area just south of the present Lauriston Road roundabout – in the south to Stamford Hill in the north, and from the Lea westward to Kingsland Road. Its nearly thirteen thousand inhabitants had just the one parish church, the recently built St John-at-Hackney. The fact that they could not all get into the church at once caused few problems, since only about one in ten adults took communion even at Easter.[1] Many of the others belonged to the many dissenting chapels that abounded in Hackney, but most were essentially unchurched.

Although church-going was such a minority activity even then, the church retained important social responsibilities. Until, towards the end of the century, the government began to accept responsibility for funding and regulating various social services, the church continued to do what it could with the charitable funds at its disposal. In Hackney, a large number of charitable trusts had been set up over the previous two hundred years with the Vicar and Churchwardens as trustees. Many of these were quite small and had very specific objects.[2] For example Heron's charity, established in 1603, directed that the income from two wooden cottages in Grove Street hamlet should be used to provide bread to the poor after church on Sundays, while the Vyner charity used the income from a house and grounds in Well Street to give coal and Christmas presents to the poor, and to establish young men in

The Prior's House, Well Street hamlet. This late-medieval building with its curious fishnet-stocking brickwork was said to have belonged before the Reformation to the Knights of St John of Jerusalem, whose name was taken by the parish. It was demolished in the early nineteenth century. Lithograph by Dean and Mundy, about 1800
Copyright: Hackney Archives Department

apprenticeships. The income from other parochial charities was intended for such miscellaneous social purposes as repairing footpaths, bridges and stiles between Clapton and Shoreditch. The parish also ran the Free and Parochial Schools and the parish almshouses, including the Monger almshouse in Well Street hamlet.

Several ancient Hackney charities bear names that are not of English origin, including the Andree, Franco and Pereira charities, and other names of non-English origin will appear frequently in this history among benefactors, clergy and parishioners. Clearly the proximity of London meant that this rural area was long ago familiar with people whose forebears came from other countries. Clearly too these immigrant families having prospered in England were keen to make some kind of contribution to local society.

Because he was at the centre of a web of social, political and religious responsibilities, the Vicar had to be carefully chosen. The authority to appoint any rector or vicar lay with the patron of the living, usually a layman, and often an aristocratic landowner. The patronage of Hackney belonged to the Tyssen family, who were until 1821 also lay rectors of Hackney; their ordained substitute, or 'vicar', was John James Watson. Watson became Rector in 1821, when the patron relinquished his rectory.

THE ORDER OF ST JOHN OF JERUSALEM

South Hackney parish church's dedication to St John of Jerusalem is most unusual. It is a misnomer in one sense – there was no such person as 'St John of Jerusalem', and the church celebrates St John the Baptist as its patron. But in medieval Europe the name of St John of Jerusalem was well known through the title of an independent and powerful order of religious, sometimes called the Knights Hospitaller.

Pilgrimage has always been a feature of religious observance, satisfying many needs. Christian pilgrims from Europe naturally wanted to go to the holy land of Palestine. Centuries ago this was hazardous: these early back-packers faced brigands, lack of banks, grasping merchants, unfamiliar illnesses and other perils. To help them, hostels were established along the pilgrim routes and in Palestine. In the late eleventh century, western Christianity extended its defence of Christendom against Islam into a series of Crusades to seize Palestine from its Muslim occupants and establish the Kingdom of Jerusalem as an outpost of western Europe. Among the institutions established during the Crusade period was a new hostel in Jerusalem dedicated to St John the Baptist and founded by Gerard around 1100.

Gerard's successor Raymond expanded the hostel's role in two ways. First, he turned the hostel into a hospital, a place where sick pilgrims could be treated. He provided for the men who ran St John's hospital in Jerusalem a Rule similar to those of orders of monks. The Rule makes clear the order's commitment to 'our lords, the sick'. Second, Raymond arranged for pilgrims to have armed escorts. This side of the work became increasingly important, and led to the order of St John of Jerusalem establishing a private army with its own castles. The grand masters of the order were warriors, and one, Roger de Moulins, died in battle. These developments were supported in the early 1180s by the formidable Lady Agnes, the real ruler of Jerusalem; she and Gerard appear in the church windows.

All this cost a lot of money. The order therefore built up in western Europe a network of almost 20,000 manors presented to it by wealthy people seeking heavenly credit. Each manor

6   *A Parish in Perspective*

paid the profit from its agricultural activities to a local commandery, which took a rake-off to pay for its own expenses and sent the rest to the national headquarters, which again took a share and sent the balance to Palestine. The national headquarters and commanderies were impressive buildings to judge from those that survive for example at Clerkenwell, Sutton-at-Hone (Kent) and near Croix de Rozon (Geneva). The property owned by the order in Well Street, South Hackney – a large, late-medieval house built of brick standing roughly where Forsyth House now stands on the Frampton Park estate – was not so pretentious but it was enough to establish the name of St John of Jerusalem in the area, ready to be taken up by the first Rector. It was demolished in the early nineteenth century

After the Reformation, the order disappeared in England, but continued to operate in Roman Catholic countries. After the Muslims regained Palestine, its base was Malta – hence the common name 'Maltese cross' for the eight-pointed white cross on a black ground which had long been its peace-time badge. In war, its knights wore a red surcoat marked with a white cross; this badge appears on one of the bosses of the chancel of South Hackney parish church. Another emblem often used by the order was the Lamb of God, an illustration of the title given to Jesus by John the Baptist; it appears four times in the church – as a boss, on a pew-end, outside over the eastern-most window, and at the top of the spire.

In nineteenth century England, interest in the Hospitaller tradition revived. The dedication of South Hackney church is one indicator of this. More significant was the establishment in 1877 of what became St John Ambulance, concerned to provide first aid training and assistance. It also set up an eye hospital in Jerusalem in 1882. The hospital continues to provide free eye treatment in Jerusalem, the West Bank and Gaza, mostly for Palestinians not covered by the Israeli health system. The British Crown recognised the revived Order and added lions and unicorns from the Royal Arms between the arms of the Maltese Cross; they can be seen in the east window of the church.

A New Parish Develops

The size of Watson's ancient parish of Hackney made it possible to believe that one reason why the poorer people of Grove Street and Well Street hamlets mostly did not trouble to walk the half-mile or so to St John-at-Hackney church was that it was too far away; or perhaps they were overawed by their social superiors who did attend. Either way, the obvious solution was to provide a separate chapel-of-ease for southern Hackney; Watson also planned to build a chapel-of-ease in the Shacklewell area of western Hackney. His intention was that practically all the seats in the new chapels would be freely available to all, so that the 'numerous poor' of these areas should not be excluded from church.[3] Land for the southern chapel was given by local businessman John De Kewer. A few gravestones still mark the site, on the north side of Well Street, almost opposite Shore Road.

Watson sent the bishop a plan of the proposed new chapel in late 1806. Its classically-inspired design had two notable features. As at the then-new St John-at-Hackney church, the main entrance would bring worshippers into the church at its side, with the altar to their right; this was the only way the portico could face Well Street and the altar face east. More remarkably, because the building was relatively small, the pulpit was to be placed at the western end, with the main seats facing into the central aisle so that worshippers could see both altar and pulpit. A gallery round three sides of the building was planned, bringing the total seating capacity to 732.[4] Appeals to raise funds for the building of the two chapels were launched, and that for the Well Street chapel quickly attracted twice what was given for Shacklewell.[5] Watson was in high hopes that the southern chapel would be ready by the summer of 1807.

But things did not go smoothly. It was 1810 before the chapel was finished, and to a rather simpler and more conventional design than that originally proposed. The nineteenth century Hackney memoirist, Dr Benjamin Clarke, remembered it as 'an extremely plain building' with space for 750 worshippers behind a typical late Georgian neo-classical façade. Between pilastered flanking walls, two Ionic pillars supported the centre of a pediment whose main, rather incongruous, point of interest was a clockface; rising above the apex of the pediment was a very un-Greek pillared drum, satisfying the need for a tower-like feature.[6] In view of the medieval presence in the area of the crusader order of the Knights Hospitallers, the new chapel was dedicated in the name of St John of Jerusalem, the common name for the order's St John the Baptist hospital in Jerusalem. This nice piece of antiquarianism probably owed much to the man who had in 1808 taken charge of church work in southern Hackney. The young Reverend Henry Handley Norris had previously been a curate of Hackney and had inherited the local Norris estate in 1804. Although the chapel had been started with funds subscribed by the public, Norris himself paid for its completion in 1810. He also gave to the chapel trustees the £20 annual income from a farm he owned in Buckinghamshire to help pay clergy to serve the chapel;[7] he himself lived off his private income, as was not uncommon for Anglican clergy in the nineteenth century.

It was not long before the growing population of Hackney justified formally splitting the ancient parish into three new parishes. In 1824, two of Watson's curates took charge of the newly-defined parishes of West Hackney and South Hackney, long, narrow strips of land along two sides of the ancient parish. George Paroissien took West Hackney; during the thirty-six years he had spent as Watson's assistant he must have given up hope of ever having a parish of his own, despite his name.[8] Norris naturally took South Hackney, covering most of the southern quarter of the ancient parish of Hackney, stretching from Hackney Wick in the east to London Fields in the west; its boundary with the new, smaller Hackney parish ran roughly where Loddiges Road, Elsdale Street and Well Street market now stand. It had a population of a little over five thousand, so the chapel-of-ease was more than adequate in size, and it became the parish church despite being a little way west of the centre of the new parish. Norris's house, lying between the traditionally linked hamlets of Grove Street and Well Street, was closer to the centre of the new parish; it is likely that Norris had influenced the boundary with this in mind. Norris continued to live in his ancestral mansion even after 1830, when William George Daniel Tyssen, the patron now of South Hackney as well as of Hackney, paid coal merchant and undertaker Nutter Gray £1800 for a large house and garden in Tryon's Place, now Tudor Road, as a parsonage for the new parish.[9] In the same year, Tyssen also provided the parish with its graveyard; it cost him £1000. The provision of the parsonage and graveyard was among the details of the financial settlement whose negotiation delayed the formal separation of the parishes until 1831.

Norris continued to co-operate closely with the clergy and lay leaders of St John-at-Hackney not only on local affairs but also as a member of the Hackney Phalanx. This was one of the most important of the influential movements organised by members of the Church of England in response to the changes they saw in society. Two of the other movements are well known: the evangelical Clapham Sect promoted a variety of social and religious reforms at the start of the century, while the later high church Oxford Movement promoted a re-discovery of the church's medieval Catholic

10   *A Parish in Perspective*

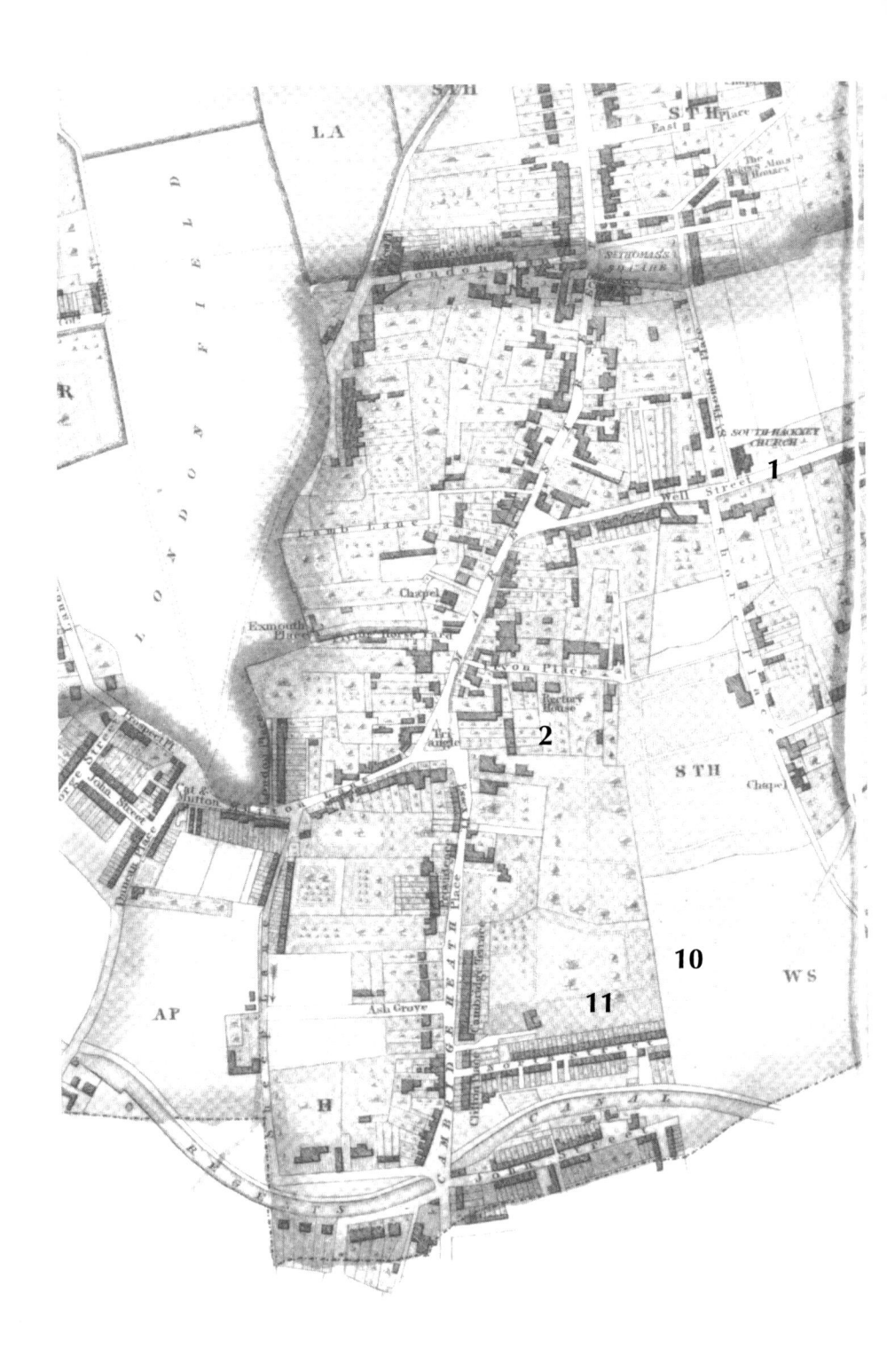

The heart of the new parish of South Hackney in 1831. The initials are those of the major landowners: Henry (Handley) Norris, Sir John Cass Charity and St Thomas's Hospital.

1 The first South Hackney church
2 the clergy house
3 Norris's mansion
4 the parochial school
5 Monger's almshouse
6 site of the school after 1847
7 site of the present church, 1848
8 site of Norris almshouse, 1852
9 site of the Rectory, built in 1870, just to the south of the present Rectory
10 site of Christ Church, Gore Road, built in 1871 (see page 53)
11 North Street, the home of Walter Southgate in the 1890s (see page 61)
12 the building that became All Saints House in 1895 (see page 75)

Ashpitel's map as revised by Edmeston, 1831 Copyright: Hackney Archives Department

1800 to 1850: From Hamlet to Fully-fledged Parish

SOUTH HACKNEY'S RECTOR PLAYS A NATIONAL ROLE: THE REV HENRY HANDLEY NORRIS MA

Henry Handley Norris's family had lived in Grove Street for over a century, owning thirty-four acres in southern Hackney but concentrating on their City business, trading with the Baltic and Russia. His ancestor Hugh Norris had moved from Somerset before the Civil War, during which he supported Cromwell against the King. The family house stood between Penshurst and Southborough Roads near where they meet Lauriston Road. Norris's great-grandfather climbed the social ladder, and his activities as a magistrate had prompted him to ensure that the new mansion he had built was robust enough to withstand attack. Perhaps growing up in a well-defended home contributed to Henry Handley Norris's sense of leading an embattled life.

Born in 1771, he attended Dr Newcombe's, the most prestigious of several private schools in Hackney, and graduated from Peterhouse, Cambridge in 1793. He succeeded to his father's estate in 1804, but by then he had embarked on a non-commercial career as an Anglican clergyman. Combining his responsibilities as landlord and as parson, he became a curate to his brother-in-law, J J Watson, vicar of St John-at-Hackney, within whose parish stood the Norris mansion. In due course, he became minister of the new chapel of ease for southern Hackney and later Rector of the new parish of South Hackney, collecting along the way canonries at Llandaff and St Paul's. He took very little of the pay to which he was entitled, saying that to do so would compromise his voluntary status. He lived instead on his private income, providing from it large subsidies for church activities in Hackney.

The early years of Norris's clerical career were overshadowed by the war with revolutionary France. Unsurprisingly therefore, as landowner and as clergyman his views were distinctly conservative. The freedoms displayed by the women of revolutionary France inspired him to publish a sermon in 1801 on *The Influence of the Female Character upon Society*, according to which women are by

The Norris family mansion standing in its park beside Grove Street, viewed from the south-east and rendered with some artistic licence. It is hard to imagine any ordinary parishioner being bold enough to call on the Rector at home.
Pencil sketch by G Toussaint, about 1840
Copyright: Hackney Archives Department

nature either more pious or more depraved than men; they have a vested interest in promoting Christianity since men, if unafraid of life after death, will mistreat and enslave them. He gave the copy now in the Hackney archives to Catherine Powell, who cannot have been too displeased with its ideas, for she married him four years later. Norris had the sermon printed by a distant cousin in Taunton; family loyalty meant a lot to him.

Already in 1793 Norris had embarked on his national career, as committee member of the Society for Promoting Christian Knowledge. Founded to distribute copies of the scriptures and liturgy, the SPCK had made relatively little impact in over a century, with the result that the British and Foreign Bible Society was started in 1804. Its rapid success enraged Norris, who in 1814 published a book that portrayed the BFBS as a threat to the established Church, despite its support from bishops and royalty. Norris also attacked the London Society for Promoting Christianity among the Jews because he felt that all available resources needed to be devoted to bolstering the loyalty of English people to their established Church. He was deeply antagonistic to Roman Catholicism and to Nonconformity, writing to the prime minister in 1813 to complain bitterly that 'There is one or other sectarian conventicle open for the purpose of poisoning the minds of the poor *every* night.'[10]

But it would be unfair to think of Norris's conservatism as merely negative. Together with the rector of Hackney and his wealthy brother Joshua Watson, he led the Hackney Phalanx to national prominence through its positive successes. Reacting to what they saw as the threat of secular or non-conformist education, the Phalanx identified the need to expand education under church control, founding the National Society for Promoting the Education of the Poor in the Principles of the Established Church throughout England and Wales in 1811. Using their connections with skill and energy, the Phalangists had brought church controlled education to tens of thousands of children by 1816. It was a remarkable achievement, and one which, ironically, strengthened the case for the state to fund and regulate education.

The Phalanx then turned its attention to improving the organisation of the church. Adding political influence to their wide network of contacts, they persuaded the Government in the midst of the post-war depression to promise the vast sum of a million pounds for building more churches particularly for the rapidly growing population of new urban areas. They were rarely beautiful buildings. Norris also campaigned for other church reforms, including the much-needed rationalisation of clergy incomes.

Norris achieved the zenith of his power between 1812 and 1827, when the prime ministership was held by one of Joshua Watson's college friends, Lord Liverpool. Norris's own political position was similar to Liverpool's Toryism, and the prime minister regularly consulted him on church affairs, particularly when a bishop was to be appointed. Norris used this influence to ensure the promotion of men sympathetic to the views of the Phalanx, capable, energetic men often selected from the upwardly mobile middle classes. He thus ensured that these views continued to count long after Liverpool was dead and he himself had lost political influence.

Norris was also chaplain to and an active associate of the Earl of Shaftesbury.

His publications, the societies he promoted and the appointments he secured show clearly where Norris stood. He feared irreligious secularisation and democracy, while he saw in non-conformist and 'popish' Christianity the threat of a return to the civil strife of earlier centuries. He genuinely believed that the greatest contentment for the greatest number was to be obtained by persuading people to accept and defend established Christianity. If that also defended the settled political order and incidentally the wealth of the Norrises, the Powells and the Watsons, that was beside the point. Whatever else he was, Norris was not consciously a cynical user of religion for political purposes. Perhaps the best evidence for this is *A Pastor's Legacy*, the book published posthumously based on the notes Norris used for the confirmation classes he gave in the last year of his life.

The Phalanx was as much a group of friends and relations living near each other as a pressure group in the modern sense, and they sometimes cooperated with people with views different from their own. Yet Norris himself was not an easy man to deal with. His part in the controversy with the BFBS was intemperate, and he had difficulties with the architects of both church and almshouse in South Hackney; he finally left the SPCK in 1834 over his high-handed approach to management. Especially in the early years of his career, he sometimes drew an amused scorn from his antagonists, one of whom exasperatedly condemned in print the 'mental mistiness' of 'the little man from South Hackney'.[11] Dissenters in Hackney much preferred to deal with JJ Watson, who was less combative in his approach to them.

For all that, his contribution to the early nineteenth century church was significant and long lasting. He and his Hackney colleagues had set the church's agenda for decades to come. His South Hackney parishioners were proud of their Rector and in 1840 presented his wife with a fine portrait of him by Thomas Phillips RA. Given by the Norris family, it hangs today in the church that is Norris's magnificent memorial, the first rector gazing out steadily from under his domed forehead, wearing his preaching bands and gown.

heritage. The Hackney Phalanx is particularly relevant to our story and deserves to be better known. Like the Claphamites it was heavily dependent on a few wealthy laymen who wanted social improvements. Like the Oxford Movement, it had a high-flown idea of the church's authority and importance, hence the term 'high church'. Its distinctive line was essentially conservative: there was no need to alter or develop the traditional teaching and liturgy of the established church, but there was an urgent need to strengthen its weakening hold on the people and to expand its activity in order to prevent economic and political change from quickly destroying all that they valued in English society. Hackney tended to oppose Clapham's initiatives because they seemed to threaten the Church of England's established status as the official religion of the country, and in turn Oxford reacted against some of Hackney's principles, especially those that they believed made the church subservient to the state. Both of the Phalanx's main nation-wide campaigns – to establish church schools and to build new churches – were eventually to be exemplified in South Hackney by the Rector who was one of its chiefs.

A Parochial School is Founded

Many thoughtful people of the time appreciated the importance of making education and training available to children whose parents were too poor or too ignorant to provide it for them. A proposal to fund parochial schools from local taxation was defeated in Parliament in 1807, and in 1810 what was to become the voluntary British and Foreign Schools Society was founded to build and run non-denominational schools for poor children. Both developments shocked Norris and his Hackney Phalanx colleagues because one way or another they would have diluted the responsibility of the established Church for education. In reaction, they founded in 1811 the ponderously named National Society for the Education of the Poor in the Principles of the Established Church throughout England and Wales.

On Norris's own patch the establishment of a school in Grove Street was his priority once he had completed the chapel of ease, spurred on no doubt by the establishment of a free school by the dissenting Calvinists of the Wells Street Chapel in 1807.[12] By 1810 a site had been identified, a corner of Norris's land straddling the footpath that then ran between the hamlets of Grove Street and Well Street, just west of where the present church was built later. Norris himself gave £600 to start the project, and he obtained from John De Kewer a further £200 that was invested to produce £10 income a year. This added to subscriptions and special chapel collections gave the school an annual income of about £120, allowing Norris to employ two teachers. The schoolmaster, Charles Williams, was paid £40 a year, which he augmented with a £20 salary as chapel clerk; his wife the schoolmistress earned £26. That Norris was able to make a gift of fifteen times a male teacher's annual salary amply demonstrates both his wealth and his generosity.

The teaching couple were supplied with a house with a school room attached at each side, one for up to sixty boys the other for thirty girls. This catered for only a small percentage of the children in the new parish. Even allowing for the sixty boys who attended the dissenting school, clearly the great majority of South Hackney's poorer children remained untouched by formal education.

Both Norris and his wife Catherine gave part-time assistance at the new school. But neither they nor the paid teachers would actually have taught many of the children, for National Society schools used the monitorial system developed in India by Andrew Bell. Older pupils, or 'monitors', were taught carefully graded lessons which they then repeated to groups of about ten younger children; all teaching was by rote. The syllabus was very narrow by today's standards. Admitted at the age of seven, the children were taught to read, write and count as well as being 'instructed in the principles of religion'. The 'charity children' were taken to church each Sunday. The girls were additionally taught plain needlework, which had the extra benefit of allowing the school to supply each pupil with some items of clothing. The children left when a job had been found for them, though parents often withdrew girls early to help with running the home, which helps explain why the school had fewer girls than boys.

In 1834, the expanding charity school needed more funds. A series of fund-raising charity sermons was started; the first, held in March 1835, was preached by Bishop Blomfield of London, after which the full congregation gave £78 for the school.[13] Norris gave an endowment of a further £550 in Bank of England annuities, and a new committee of management was established, most of its members to be selected by the Rector from among those who made a one guinea subscription. At this time, the purpose and methods of the school were set out in some detail. Among other things, the children were to be 'taught to read their bibles, to say their prayers morning and evening, to repeat the Church catechism and to perform their other religious duties according to the tenets of the Established Church of England' in order that they 'may be trained to habits of religion and industry so as to qualify them for respectable service.'[14] It was not, it seems, a school where youngsters were to be encouraged to think for themselves.

Scenes of Clerical Life

We are fortunate to have a glimpse of South Hackney church life in the late 1820s in letters written to his father by one of Norris's assistant ministers, John May.[15] In 1828, this young priest came to South Hackney from Bures, a large but poor country parish in Suffolk, hoping no doubt both to be more useful in a developing London suburb and to find advancement in his clerical career. Becoming one of the curates under a Rector who was as influential and wealthy as Norris and who was also understood to be the author of the anonymous *A Manual for the Parish Priest*, a popular handbook for young clergy, must have given May cause to hope for an experience that would be enriching in every way. Unfortunately, he did not find it so.

May did not at first find the company of many of his social equals. He wrote that the 'large congregation' was 'of the lower grade, with a few exceptions', since the 'higher orders, what there be of them, are regular attendands at the Great Church', that is, at St John-at-Hackney. This seems to confirm that the ease that the chapel provided was in fact mostly social rather than geographical in nature. 'I must own I wish it were otherwise', he added rather sadly.

May was disappointed in his job as well as in the opportunities for socialising. He had hoped to engage with his parishioners, at least on a professional level. Instead, he told his father, 'I have only one person in my district, who is anxious of availing herself of any assistance or advice I may be able to afford.' This seems to have been typical, for he reports of Norris that 'he himself says he knows but few of his parishioners, for it happens not here, as it happened to me at Bures, that either the incumbent or his curate, becomes intimately acquainted with his flock individually.' But of course, Bures was in deepest Suffolk where traditional connections and social pressures were still in place; the poorer classes who had moved to Hackney to be closer to London had cut themselves loose of many of the ties that bound them to their parish church.

A few months after his arrival, the Rector suggested he might have a post at St Thomas's Hospital, a job which paid £180 a year, £40 more than his curacy in South Hackney. The post offered to May seems to have been in the gift of Norris, since it was currently held by another ex-curate of South Hackney, Challis Paroissien, the son of George Paroissien, first Rector of West Hackney. The job-offer to May was probably a case of Norris adopting the usual Hackney Phalanx approach: find a young man with potential, try him out in a challenging job, and then, if he shines, place his foot firmly on the ladder to preferment with the offer of a well-paid and influential post. May however turned the job down, possibly mistaking the point he had reached on the Phalanx career plan – he felt he had made a good impression on Norris and at first rather naively thought the post offered was worth £500 a year. He thus found himself in South Hackney for another five years. He eventually married Maria Frampton, a member of the wealthy family commemorated in the name of Frampton Park Road, off Well Street. They left London, and May ended his career in charge of a country parish.

Norris's aloofness from his parishioners is further evidenced by a revealing incident in 1824 which Norris himself reported to Bishop Howley. Charles Williams, who had been the chapel clerk and school master until about 1820 and who had since then given his services as clerk without payment, was discovered by Norris to have been 'for a length of time in regular attendance at seven in the morning and in the evening at the prayer meeting of an Independent Conventicle in the Parish; and I found that this attendance was a matter of public notoriety and public conversation.' Norris forthwith dismissed Williams as clerk and barred him from communion.[16] Whether the bishop wondered how Norris could have been unaware of a cause of scandal under his nose for so long we do not know.

The Church Charities

The administration of the many charities run by the church had sometimes been haphazard during the eighteenth century, when the Vicar and Churchwardens had somehow lost control of the Monger Almshouse in Well Street hamlet. The almshouse had been built in 1669 under the terms of Henry Monger's will to house six men 'of the age of sixty years or thereabouts' to be appointed by the Vicar and Churchwardens for 'the term of their natural lives if they continued civil, honest men'. During the eighteenth century, these appointments had come to be made, without any legal justification, by the trustees of the neighbouring independent Cass charity. Using a discretion that Monger's will had not given anyone, the Cass trustees led by Dame Elizabeth Cass not only permitted the almsmen to have their wives with them, but even allowed these wives to stay on as widows. When the church regained control of the almshouse in 1800, such humane infractions of the letter of Monger's will were corrected: the widows were ejected. It was harsh that the women of southern Hackney were treated in this way, particularly because when in 1679 Monger's original bequest proved inadequate for the

Four of the six houses of the original Monger's Almshouses, built in 1669 and replaced in 1847. The picture exaggerates the size of the houses.
Pen and wash drawing, about 1790
Copyright: Hackney Archives Department

maintenance of the almshouse and the payment of the almsmen's pensions, it was a woman, Joanna Martin, who came to the rescue. She gave the Monger trustees two wooden cottages on the land to the west of the almshouse, the rental income from which was to make up the shortfall.[17]

A similar rather unimaginative narrowing of view can be detected in the approach taken by people setting up church charities in Hackney after 1800. In the relatively broadminded eighteenth century, Jeremiah Marlowe in his will of 1764 left money to help 'industrious, sober, honest and deserving' poor householders, and directed that 'no such housekeeper be paid or refused ... on account of any religious or political opinion'.[18] But the income from the South Sea annuities bought in 1818 with a large legacy from the ever-generous John De Kewer was to be used on 1st February each year to buy coal and potatoes only for 'every poor inhabitant of Grove Street and Well Street and the parts adjacent, who should regularly attend divine service at St John's chapel, and should attend no other place of worship.' No doubt this was in part an attempt to give poor people an extra incentive to return to the Anglican church rather than attending one of the burgeoning dissenting chapels; it is just as likely to have had quite the opposite effect.

The splitting of the ancient parish required new arrangements to be made for the administration of the charities that had hitherto been the responsibility of the Rector and Churchwardens of Hackney. Initially, the Rector of Hackney and his newly promoted colleagues seem to have handled the matter informally, using a common-sense approach: if the charity is localised in a particular parish, like Monger's almshouse, let it be administered by that parish; otherwise administer charitable assets jointly and share the income roughly in proportion to the populations of the three parishes. In 1833, the Church Commissioners for Building New Churches put this arrangement on an official basis, giving Hackney parish half the income from the joint assets and dividing the other half equally between West and South Hackney.[19]

The efforts of the local clergy to assist the poor were not confined to the administration of the parochial charities. Norris was president, and other clergy officers, of the Hackney Friendly Society, formed in 1829 'to encourage among the Working Classes of Society ... habits of industry, forethought and self-support, by affording them the means of assuring a provision for Infancy, Old Age, Sickness and Burial.' The contributions of the 130 members went wholly into the common insurance fund; the honorary members, including Norris, paid the administrative expenses. Human nature being what it is, members sometimes tried to take improper advantage of the scheme; members were occasionally expelled for offering 'frivolous excuses for drawing on the funds.'

A Bundle of Receipts

By some obscure but happy chance, a bundle of receipts for money paid by South Hackney church in 1842 and 1843 has survived.[20] They shed fascinating sidelights on the daily life of the church at that time.

Apart from the Rector and his assistant curates, several lay people were employed by South Hackney parish. According to the receipts, the annual paybill for them was this:

Beadle, Charles Evans	£30.0.0
Sexton, Richard Steib	£25.0.0
Organist and Choirmaster, George Styfield	£25.0.0
Vestry Clerk, Charles Pulley	£20.0.0
Pew opener, Ann Rawbone	£5.5.0
Pew opener, Elizabeth Butler	£5.5.0
Organ blower, Thomas Butler	£3.3.0

The pew-openers' and organ blower's jobs were obviously part-time, but it is not clear from the receipts which if any of the others were full-time employees. It is illuminating however to compare the pay of these lay people both with John May's £140 salary as a curate fifteen years earlier and with the schoolmaster-cum-clerk's £60 total salary a few years before that.

The duties of Beadle Evans would have been similar to those ascribed by Charles Dickens to Mr Bumble in *Oliver Twist*, which was published in 1837. Like his fictional counterpart, Evans had an imposing uniform provided by the parish, and, because it was bought in the year for which we have the receipts, we know what it looked like and how much it cost. His indoor uniform, including a scarlet waistcoat, was decorated with gilt buttons and two yards of gold lace; this together with gaiters and cotton drawers cost the parish £7.10.0. For going around the parish, Evans was supplied with a greatcoat costing five pounds, and to top it all he had a beadle's hat, again decorated with gold lace, which cost £2.8.0. He must have been an impressive sight, wearing an outfit that had cost almost six months' salary. We must hope it lasted a good many of the remaining forty-one of the fifty-two years he spent as beadle of the parish.

The Clerk and legal advisor, Charles Horton Pulley, was wealthy enough to live in the eastern half of Sutton House, for he combined his duties as Clerk to South Hackney parish with several other jobs. Dr Clarke remembered him as a regular 'pluralist in all legal clerkly parochial offices.' He was also remembered as the Clerk who was supposed to have tried to horsewhip a stubborn Vestryman into line! Certainly his almost illegible handwriting, scrawled hugely across the parish records of the 1840s and '50s, suggests the arrogance necessary for such behaviour.[21]

George Styfield had been appointed as organist only in the summer of

1842. As well as playing the organ for services, his duties included instructing the boys of the charity school in Psalmody. The post had been advertised in the *Times*, so his appointment was a very public affair, which with the salary offered suggests that organ music was regarded by Norris as an important part of church services.

Other invoices provide otherwise unrecorded details of church life. We know that surplices were worn because Ann Rawbone the pew opener washed them for 2/6 each. A dozen bottles of communion wine cost £2.2.0, and the church appears to have used almost two bottles of it every time Holy Communion was celebrated, which tells us something about the congregation. At Christmas, the church was decked with boughs of holly; they were collected by Richard Steib the sexton in addition to his other duties, for which he was paid an extra £1.10.0.

Direct comparisons between today's prices and those shown by the receipts and other church records of the 1830s and 1840s is misleading because of changes in technology, life style, social values and taxation. However, the receipts tell us that church cleaners were paid 3/6 a day in 1842, which allows us to translate prices in the 1840s records into the number of days' unskilled

An unflattering view of a parish beadle in his official dress – and certainly not based on Charles Evans, beadle of South Hackney, whose outfit was not bought until 1842. Engraving by George Cruikshank for The Gentleman's Magazine, *1829*

1800 to 1850: From Hamlet to Fully-fledged Parish

work required to pay them. Since a cleaner in South Hackney now earns about £50 a day, we can give the modern prices of similar items in terms of days of unskilled work. The comparison is illuminating, showing for example that, while wine was ten times more expensive then than now, a large house with a large garden in South Hackney cost about the same.

Church Services

The successor of the Hackney Phalanx at the head of the 'High-Church' party in the Church of England was the Oxford Movement, which began in 1833. Since the heyday of Lord Liverpool and the Phalanx had come to an end in 1828, several developments had given anxiety and pain to high-churchmen, among them the restoration of civil rights to Catholics in 1829 and the passing of the great Reform Act of 1832, which significantly reduced the political power of the Tories and of the established order in general. The old easy relationship between High-Church Anglicanism and government was finished, and frustration with the loss of power this implied introduced a new factionalism into Anglican church politics. The Oxford Movement was the reaction to these developments; it saw the need for a new source for the Church of England's authority and found it in its Catholic heritage.

Norris could see that the unity of his beloved Church of England was under threat as never before. He published a sermon which he had preached at South Hackney in 1842[22] in which he suggested that one of the most important sources of unity within the Church of England was its Book of Common Prayer. But it could only continue to be a source of unity if church services strictly followed the words and instructions it contained. So his sermon outlined the changes he intended to introduce in the services at South Hackney to ensure close adherence to the prayer book; it thus tells us a great deal about services at South Hackney in the 1840s.

The normal Sunday morning service was Morning Prayer followed immediately by the first part of the Holy Communion service and a sermon. Once a month, the Communion service would be completed after the sermon, with confirmed church members receiving communion; those not entitled to take communion would leave after the sermon. Throughout the Sunday morning service, the minister would wear one of the long flowing white surplices kept clean by Ann Rawbone, a symbol both of the worshipful nature of the morning service and of the pastoral relationship between minister and congregation. Norris saw Evening Prayer, the Sunday afternoon service, as something different: here, the minister was a more of a lecturer than a pastor, and as such would wear his black preaching gown.

Norris thought it would be best to carry out the baptism of infants as part of the Sunday morning service, but acknowledged that that service was already very long, being 'compounded of two parts originally separate.' Nevertheless, he told his congregation, 'it shall be my endeavour to win your cordial assent and concurrence to its gradual restoration' to its place in the main Sunday service. Until then, baptisms would take place in the context of Morning or Evening Prayer on weekdays. This certainly shows that Norris was able to accommodate the resistance to change that congregations showed then no less than now. One change in congregational habits however he was prepared to push for quite hard: he thought it both unscriptural and inappropriate for church-goers to sit while prayers were being said – he told them they should be on their knees.

The New Church is Built

Persuaded by the Hackney Phalanx among others that there were too few Church of England places of worship, the government paid for a massive Anglican church building programme, starting in 1818. In one sense, the efforts of the Phalanx and their Church Building Society were misguided: they made it their aim to provide a seat in an established Anglican church for every person living in each parish, but there is no reason to think that more people wished to attend church than there were seats for them. Even had demand for church places outstripped supply, it would have been easy to deal with the situation – as Roman Catholics did later – by holding extra services in the same building. Nevertheless, during the middle years of the century, two new Anglican churches on average were being opened every week, usually in the gothic style. Perhaps the desire to assert the Anglican establishment's power was an important motive behind this massive effort, and certainly the multiplicity of often poorly-constructed buildings faced later generations with many difficulties and hard choices. Still, what followed all this activity was reasonably encouraging, since attendance at Anglican churches increased somewhat faster than the population.

For much of his ministry in South Hackney, Norris had needed to give attention to his national responsibilities as a chief of the Hackney Phalanx, adviser on church affairs to the prime minister and committee member of the Society for Promoting Christian Knowledge; in any case, the old chapel-of-

ARCHITECTURAL THEORIST AND CHURCH ARCHITECT: EDWARD CHARLES HAKEWILL, FRIBA

This feature is indebted to an unpublished treatise on the Hakewill family by Bob Hakewill.

The architect of St John of Jerusalem church, Edward Charles Hakewill, divided his career mostly between part-time local government appointments in London and restoring medieval churches. Only in Hackney was he given the opportunity to design churches from scratch; as well as St John of Jerusalem, he was responsible for St James's church at Clapton and for the now-demolished church St Michael and All Angels London Fields. Of these, St John of Jerusalem is undoubtedly the most impressive, designed when the architect was only 27 years old.

His precocity is understandable. Born into an architectural family in 1816, by the age of 14 he was already working with his brother in their father's architectural office, learning his profession by practising it. At 20, encouraged by his architect-uncle, he boldly entered the competition to design the Houses of Parliament. Yet his first executed independent design was not a building at all but the 1838 memorial statue in Reading. His connection with Hackney began around the same time, when he attempted to obtain the commission to design the new chapel of ease for Dalston, to be dedicated to St Philip. He was unsuccessful but seems to have impressed the Rector of Hackney, Dr J J Watson, who gave him the commission for St James's church at Clapton in 1839. The young Hakewill was naturally proud of his success and exhibited his design for St James's, along with other drawings, at the Royal Academy in the early 1840s.

During these years Hakewill was carrying out the research which led in 1851 to the publication of his only book, *The Temple*, an illustrated essay about the design of Noah's Ark, Moses' desert Tabernacle and the successive Temples in Jerusalem. Despite the careful piecing together of the details of ancient structures real and mythical, the book strikes the modern reader as rather curious, and not merely for the literal way the Old Testament myths are interpreted. Hakewill finds a parallel between the design development of these pre-Christian structures and that of Christian churches. As the ancient structures culminated in the classical Hellenistic design of the Temple built by Herod the Great, which Jesus knew, so Christian church architecture develops from the Roman basilica, through the Romanesque and Norman to its culmination in 'pointed', or gothic, architecture.

This approach was very much of-a-piece with what other writers were saying at the time, and like them Hakewill makes no effort to soften his condemnation of those who built churches after the design of Greek temples. He does however add a curious detail to the condemnation: churches based on Greek temple design had no side doors, whereas a church that is true to itself must have side doors since Noah's Ark had them! The main axis of a church, from main west door past the font to the sanctuary and altar, Hakewill derives from the plan of Moses' tabernacle. Hakewill's book also expresses strong opinions about the use of statuary in churches. Despite idealising medieval architecture as *the* Christian architecture, he has no patience with statues which could be mistaken for idols and thus pollute and desecrate the House of God; he specifically condemns even statues 'in the form of the Saviour on the cross' of the kind which were so common in medieval churches.[23]

Such developing opinions would certainly have made Hakewill attractive to the fiercely anti-Catholic Rector of South Hackney who wanted a fine new gothic church to replace the old Greek-style church in Well Street. Having been given the commission for St John of Jerusalem church, Hakewill designed it very much in line with the principles he was refining as he continued his researches.

Hakewill was never again to have the green field site and generous budget given him by Norris in South Hackney. We must hope that he did not find his subsequent work too tedious. Much of it involved the restoration of medieval churches in Essex and Suffolk, and the frequent removal of Georgian accretions from these churches would no doubt have pleased the author of *The Temple*.

> Hakewill eventually moved into a house he had designed at Playford, near Ipswich, in 1867. Unfulfilling as his career may in the end have been, he was comfortably off: the Playford household included a coachman, footman, cook and housemaid. He died at Playford in 1872, and a window in his memory can still be seen in the nearby church of Rushmere St Andrew, which he himself had largely rebuilt in 1861.
>
> Nikolaus Pevsner, the great critic of English architecture, had little time for Hakewill's work, regarding some of his restorations as essentially destructive and much of his original work as 'more curious than good'. Yet there can be little doubt that but for the reasonably sympathetic restorations of Hakewill and other Victorians, many English mediaeval churches would have fallen irretrievably into ruin. And, for all its academic unoriginality, St John of Jerusalem at least shows that Hakewill could rise to the occasion and produce a bold and impressive design.

ease in Well Street had been adequate for the population of South Hackney, especially after it had been enlarged and embellished in 1818. By the beginning of the 1840s, the seventy-year-old Rector was able to devote more of his time and energy to his parish. He realised that even if the chapel was adequate now, the time was coming when the fields and market gardens of South Hackney would be buried under working class terraces and middle class villas, greatly increasing the population and, as the conventional wisdom had it, requiring more church accommodation.

Norris began his public campaign to build a new church for South Hackney with a meeting in the parochial school in May, 1842.[24] He claimed that the existing chapel was in need of expensive repairs, and that in any case it held only six hundred people. He was exaggerating: the thirty year old chapel may possibly have been poorly built and badly maintained, but even in 1810 it was supposed to have been big enough to hold 750 worshippers, and it had since been enlarged. Norris had no difficulty over the following two years in persuading a great range of people to make donations to his church building fund. The names of the Queen Dowager, the Archbishop of Canterbury and several other bishops rubbed shoulders with those of humble parishioners in the published list of subscribers; there were even a few anonymous donations. Appropriately, Norris's project was given £1000 from the government's church building fund and £500 by the Church Building Society. The sale of materials from the old chapel once it was demolished realised a further £700.[25] The Rector himself gave £600, and his son Henry Norris gave the site for the proposed church, which he had bought for £550.

Norris selected as his architect the 26-year-old Edward Charles Hakewill, whose work on St James's church in nearby Clapton he had seen. A decade earlier, perhaps the architectural style chosen would have been Tudor Perpendicular as used for the Houses of Parliament, but by the mid-1840s the fashion had changed in favour of the 'pointed' style of around 1300. Stone was to be used, not least because to build a church in brick would have been regarded as parsimonious as well as inauthentic. Hakewill's ambitious design was soon complete, and he produced a fine perspective drawing of the proposed building. However, his estimate of the cost of the structure proved to be distinctly optimistic. In August 1844, Norris wrote to a friend, 'I have received this morning a communication from Mr Hakewill which exceedingly disappoints me. ... He writes me word that the Bricklayers and Masons works exceed his estimate by about £2000 and accordingly he subjoins a list of deductions ...' Norris feared that to make the suggested modifications would 'reduce [the church] to a rather trumpery concern', which was not at all his intention.[26] More funds were raised so that in the end most of Hakewill's 'list of deductions' were restored; the only significant exception was the vaulting that had been intended to cover the crossing. It may be that Norris hoped, in vain as it turned out, that even this part of the design could one day be realised, which would explain both why the crossing has what looks like a temporary roof when compared with the rest of the building and why the nave ends in a massive but essentially purposeless arch.

Work began at the very end of 1844, and in May of the following year the foundation stone was laid following a service in the soon-to-be-demolished old church. Among those in the procession to its successor were Hakewill and the builders. Curiously, the inscription on the foundation stone was not put there until 1852.

Once work on the structure had been started, Norris turned his attention to yet more fund-raising, about which even he claimed to feel diffident. Having raised £10000 for the structure, he now sought money for the furniture, stained glass, bells and decoration. His appeal identifies the Church of England as the ideal middle way even in aesthetic matters, for his aim is to avoid 'all superfluous and trifling additions' without falling short in completing 'the outward tokens due to Him'. For, he goes on, 'this character, we

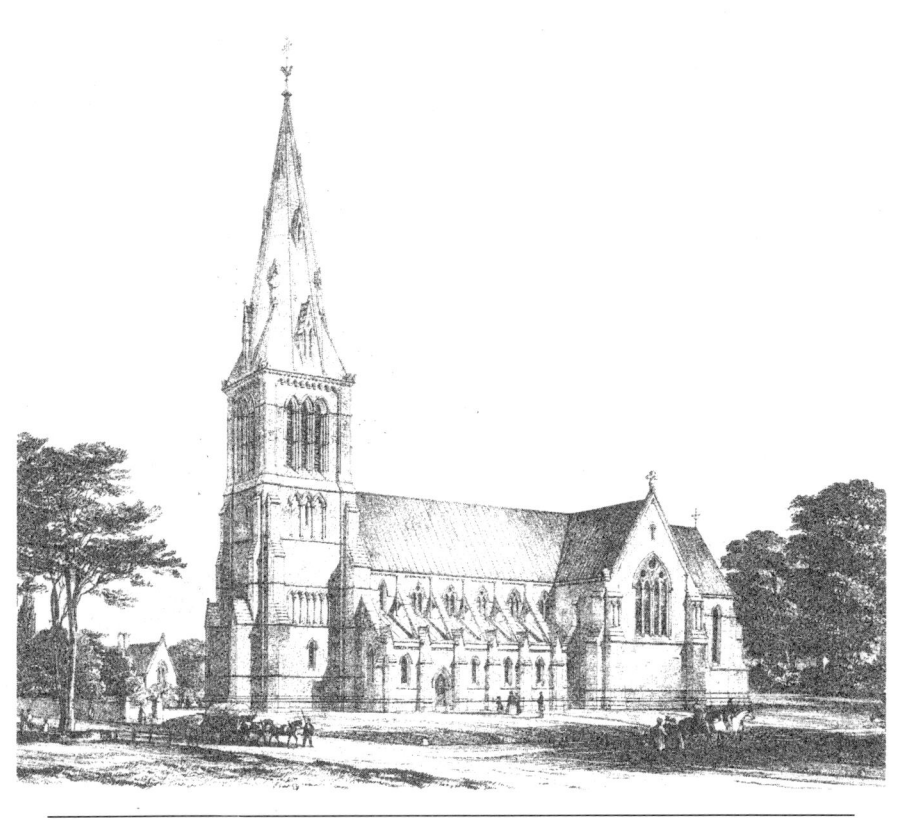

The proposed church of St John of Jerusalem, South Hackney. The tiny window at the top of the transept gable was intended to provide light in the space above the planned stone vault; because the vault proved unaffordable, the window was not built.
Lithograph by the architect, E C Hakewill, 1845
Courtesy of the Rector

trust, has been preserved in the Churches of our land where public zeal has not been wanting; distinguishing them alike from the grotesque and unseemly style of furniture which often obscures the building and distracts the attention of the worshipper, in Roman Catholic churches, and from the poverty and meanness of the bare walls, in those countries where the Reformation kept no such happy mean as in our own.'[27] In the end this further appeal raised £6000, bringing the total cost of the new church to £16000. It is interesting to compare this sum with the £2000 that local Catholics spent in these same years on building and decorating their new church at the other end of King Edward's Road.[28]

The finished church was generally praised in the architectural press. *The Builder* wrote,[29] 'Throughout the whole, "truthfulness" has been systematically adhered to: there is no deal stained to look like oak; no "cast" ornament; no plaster groin, scored and coloured to look like (how unlike!) stone. ... Where plastering appears as a covering to the rough stone (no bricks have been used) there is no attempt to make it look other than it is.' Yet there were complaints too[30] – that the flying buttresses and nave arch were architecturally unnecessary, that the nave was too wide compared with the side aisles, that the main west door was more elaborate than appropriate for the rest of the building, that there were too many bays in the nave, and that the apsidal east end could never be as satisfying as a fine east window.

Some of the praise as well as the criticism was misguided. Hakewill was carrying out an exercise in imitation. It was not until William Butterfield's revolutionary design of 1850 for brick-built All Saints', Margaret Street in the West End that Victorian gothic became creative in its own right; St John of Jerusalem was meant to look as much like a genuine medieval church as possible. Hakewill therefore selected elements of various medieval churches and put them together in a harmonious composition. For example, the tower and spire were modelled on those of Stamford parish church in Lincolnshire, and the chancel arcade and the inner plane of tracery in the clerestory on those at Stone, Kent, while the chancel vault bears a striking similarity to the one at Tidmarsh in Berkshire.[31] The composition of these elements was subject to certain over-riding considerations, the most significant of which seem to have been that as many of the congregation as possible must have a clear view of the altar and of the preacher, and that some free – that is, not pew-rented – seats should be near the front. This led Hakewill to produce a nave that he would have known was in medieval terms 'too wide'. But equally, medieval builders quite often covered perfectly good stonework with plaster that they then painted 'to look like (how unlike!) stone'.

The design of the nave arcade tells us a lot about Hakewill. The final western bay is shorter than the rest, making its arches lower in consequence, and while the two upper, or clerestory, windows of that bay are smaller and less elaborate than those in the rest of the nave, they are at least the same; by contrast, the clerestory windows that face each other across the penultimate bay are quite different from each other. It is also noteworthy that the change from octagonal to round pillars happens at a different place on each side, while the clerestory windows, and arcade capitals, corbels and mouldings are decorated in slightly different ways. All this bears witness to Hakewill's attention to detail and willingness to take trouble; it would have been easier to produce a boringly uniform arcade, and no-one would have complained if he had. But he would have known that the designers of medieval churches often employed gratuitous subtle asymmetry; the difference between the two side portals of the west front of Notre Dame de Paris is a famous example. Hakewill may well have had this idea in mind when he designed not only the odd clerestory windows, but also the unmatched transept windows. The chancel vaulting bosses suggest the same attention to detail; mere chance would surely not have made them so similar to the bosses of the St John's Gate, Clerkenwell, the still-surviving remains of the English headquarters of the Order of St John of Jerusalem.

Hakewill would also have known that medieval churches developed over the centuries as funds were available and donations were made; when a new window here or door there was put in, architectural fashions had often changed. Perhaps Hakewill was imitating the result of this process when he produced the design for the supposedly over-elaborate main door. It is less easy to explain the narrowing of the final nave arches, deliberate as it was; perhaps Hakewill knew that a similar slowing up of the arcade rhythm occurs at the west end of the great gothic cathedral at Chartres. Most subtly of all, Hakewill, or perhaps his stone-carver, hid a small face in the foliage of one of the brackets in the nave; whether this was suggested by the ancient tradition of the 'green man' or by the features of someone involved in the building we cannot know. Gruesome rather than subtle is the representation of John the Baptist's head lying on its platter which appears on one of the corbels of the arcade.

The inner faces of the great arch between the nave and the crossing were adorned with painted texts, as were the chancel arcade and the crossing roof. There was clearly some enthusiasm for texts on the walls in this very unmedieval fashion; the only ones that have survived are in the gallery over the vestibule, where the Lord's Prayer and the Ten Commandments are painted on sheets of metal fixed to the wall.

Norris, his 'good clear voice ... distinctly heard over the whole of this large Church', assisted Bishop Blomfield of London at the consecration in July 1848. It was an impressive service, with every one of the 1500 or so seats occupied, two hundred of them by robed clergy. As, to the sound of bells pealing in the tower of the new church, he led the congregation down Grove Street for a great reception in the grounds of his mansion, the Rector, now in his seventy-eighth year, must have felt particularly blessed to have been spared long enough to see his church completed. What the many local dissenters, Catholics and others disaffected towards the Church of England felt

A charmingly naive drawing of the interior of the church in the 1860s. Notice particularly the free benches in the central aisle, the position of the font, the lighting and the texts on the walls.
© Crown Copyright NMR

THE *ILLUSTRATED LONDON NEWS* SHOWS ITS READERS ROUND THE NEW CHURCH

Extracts from the *Illustrated London News*, 17 May 1845 and 22 July 1848

The new Church (dedicated to St. John of Jerusalem) is ... in the style of the best period of Pointed Architecture – 13th and 14th centuries: it is cruciform in plan; the tower and stone spire at the west end, rise to the height of nearly 200 feet; the spire is well-proportioned, being about equal in height to the tower; it has three tiers of graceful lights, and broaches supporting the Four Evangelists, beneath canopies placed at the four angles. The principal entrance beneath the tower is by a deeply recessed arched double doorway, with centre column; above is a pointed arcade, and the belfry storey has in each face a recessed triplet, surmounted by a corbel table and enriched cornice. ... The nave has side aisles with flying buttresses to the clerestory; each of the transepts is lit by a magnificent window, about 20 feet high; the choir has an apsidal end, and is lit by seven lancet windows. The length of the entire edifice is about 200 feet. The materials are Kentish rag and Speldhurst stone.

This very handsome Church is, perhaps, one of the best examples of the modern skill in church architecture which we have lately had occasion to notice. ... Passing through the west doorway, which is in the centre of a lofty tower, a square vestibule formed in the tower is entered, and separated from the church by a screen of open arches, above which is the organ gallery, supported by massive brackets of timber of extremely bold design. Doors in the screen give ingress into the Church, and its beautiful design at once arrests the eye.

The edifice is divided into a nave, with aisles; and a chancel, separated from the nave by transepts. The nave is partitioned from the aisles by five pillars, carrying six arches, above which rise the clerestory. The pillars are not of uniform shape – some of them being octangular, and others circular; and a very good diversity of ornament has been studied in the details of the capitals. ...

In the spandrills between the arches are richly sculptured brackets supporting the clustered pillars, whence spring the arches of the roof.

The clerestory windows are of varied design and character, and are all filled with stained glass, as are also the windows of the aisles.

The roof, of open work, is of excellent style, and of extremely lofty pitch, it being sixty feet in the highest point from the pavement. The arched and foliated ribs supporting the roof are of massive construction, and a degree of enrichment is given by the bolt-heads at intervals around them. At the intersection of the nave and transepts is a stone arch, of corresponding pitch to the ribs of timber just mentioned.

A striking and most effective portion of the church is the meeting of the transepts, chancel, and nave. From piers of clustered columns spring richly moulded arches, spanning the before-mentioned parts of the edifice; and from short octagonal columns, at the angles, rise groins for timber meeting in the centre, the spaces between the groins being filled with timber, and painted; whilst by the sides of the groins texts are painted, which were selected by the Rector, to illustrate the will of God, that in all times there should be a place set apart for his worship. The transepts have timber roofs; and, with the exception of large windows, of good design, filled with stained glass, are unornamented. ...

The chancel is of stone, the roof being of the same solid substance as the walls. In plan, the chancel terminates with an apse, forming a portion of an octagon, at the corners of which and sides of the chancel are columns, whence spring groins, meeting at the centre of the roof. Tall, narrow, single-light windows are in each compartment of the walls, and beneath them an arcade of trefoil-headed arches is introduced. In the panels of the arcades in the apse, the walls are painted, and adorned with diapering. In the centre or eastern compartment, the wall is blue, powdered with stars, and the inscription, 'Peace and goodwill towards men,' painted on it; whilst the north-east wall is red, diapered with fleur-de-lis, and the sacred monogram 'IHS.' The text 'He was known to them in breaking of bread,' is painted on it, as are also the Creed and the Lord's Prayer. The south-east wall is enriched with the same diapering as the opposite corner, with the commandments and the text 'When I see the blood I will pass over you.' In the north wall of the chancel within one of the arches of the arcade is an arched recess, somewhat resembling in form the memorials of the founders of churches to be met with in our old ecclesiastical structures; on the keystones of which two angels are sculptured, one of them pointing upwards, as if to say, 'He is not here; He is risen.' This recess forms the table of prothesis, or table on which the sacramental elements are placed, previous to consecration. ...

The pulpit and reading-desk are on either side of the chancel arch, and entrance to them is attained by the steps leading to the chancel. They are of admirable design and workmanship. The pulpit is of octagonal form, and the whole surface covered with diapering, elegantly wrought. The reading-desk is of open-worked arches, and has fronts looking westward and southward, the spandrills being filled with diapering. Many of the seats are free; and others have doors to them, as pews; while all have floreated ends. The last seats at the western end of the Church have very highly enriched bench ends; and on the buttresses are different devices – one having the crest of the rector, a stag pierced with an arrow; another, the lamb with a flag; the third an eagle; and the fourth a lynx, as symbolical of Christian watchfulness. The backs of these seats are very elegantly ornamented with panels and quatrefoils. ...

The windows in this Church are filled with stained glass, all of it of very meritorious design. The chancel windows contain, in small compartments, the incidents in the life of our Saviour, figures of the Apostles, &c., executed with great depth and brilliancy of colour, by Wailes, of Newcastle. The windows in the transepts are by Messrs. Powell, and represent in the tracery of the north window Abraham offering up Isaac; and, in the south, scenes in the life of Moses typical of the Redeemer, such as Moses striking the rock, Moses with the Laws, and lifting up the Serpent in the Wilderness. The remaining portions of the windows are filled with richly diapered glass. The aisle windows are simply but elegantly diapered, with the exception of two at the western end of the aisle, which have separate subject in them. ... The clerestory windows are of various design and character; one of them is a memorial window, placed there in lieu of erecting a monument to a little child, and in it are represented Christ blessing little children, and raising Jairus' daughter. This window, which is exquisitely painted, is the production of Messrs Ward and Nixon; and by the same gentlemen are two clerestory windows, con-

> taining scriptural subjects. The clerestory windows on the north side contain, in single lights, figures of Elias and John the Baptist; then, in double lights, the Royal arms of England; the arms of the sees of Canterbury, London, &c., ...
>
> In front of the altar-rails the floor is laid with Minton's tiles. The font, placed near the western end, is beautifully sculptured; it is not, however, from the design of Mr Hakewill, but was presented to the Church. The organ is from the old church at Hackney. Of the peal of bells, eight in number, one was given by the Archbishop of Armagh; another by Mr Bowdler [and the Rev Mr Laprimaudaye]; and we believe some others are also gifts.
>
> From this brief description it will be imagined the Church is one of no ordinary beauty or interest, and that the greatest praise is due to its architect, Edward C. Hakewill Esq., for so admirable a specimen of his talents.

can only be guessed at; it is hard to imagine that, for them, the vast and costly new church proclaimed much more than the power and wealth of established Anglicanism.

Another New Building: The Parochial School

The new church was not the only building project that the ageing Rector had in hand in the late 1840s. The original school buildings were not big enough for the 137 boys and 63 girls now enrolled. In any case the site was needed as part of the churchyard of the new church. At first it was intended to build the new school on a site adjacent to the church, but there was insufficient space; the site was subsequently used for the four Belle Vue cottages, now 27 to 30 Church Crescent, the rental income from which helped to fund the school.

Instead, the trustees of St Thomas's Hospital, a local landowner, gave the larger site at the end of Greenwood's Row, later Percy Road and now Kingshold Road, where the parochial school still stands. In 1847 the committee of management signed a contract with local builder William Norris – no relation of the Rector – for the erection of a new school. The cost was to be £1467, to be partially funded by the National Society, which by this time was

SOUTH HACKNEY PAROCHIAL SCHOOLS.

THE

REPORT OF THE COMMITTEE OF MANAGEMENT,

WITH THE

Treasurer's Accounts,

LIST OF SUBSCRIBERS, AND PRESENT STATE OF THE SCHOOLS,

FOR THE YEAR 1847.

Sketch of the New School Buildings.

Committee of Management for the Year 1848.

THE REV. H. H. NORRIS, M. A. RECTOR .. REV. G. P. LOCKWOOD, B. A. CURATE .. REV. T. P. WRIGHT, M. A.

Trustees.

MR. A. POWELL .. MR. J. CROWFOOT .. MR. J. CROWFOOT, JUN.

Committee.

MR. G. CHILD	MR. R. DAVIES	MR. W. D. JACKSON	MR. C. B. STUTFIELD
CAPTAIN CLARK	MR. J. D. FRAMPTON	MR. G. R. LONGDEN	MR. H. TURNER
MR. R. COMBER	MR. T. GILLESPY	MR. J. PULLEY	DR. WILLIAMS
MR. T. CRAVEN	MR. J. C. GOODIER	MR. C. R. RANDALL	MR. F. WILSON

Ladies' Committee.

MRS. NORRIS .. MRS. LOCKWOOD .. MRS. GIBSON .. MISS M. FRAMPTON .. MISS J. FRAMPTON .. MISS J. A. JONES

Auditors.—MR. G. CHILD, *Tryon's Place* .. MR. E. JONES, *London Field.*

Treasurer.—MR. E. H. JONES, *Well Street.*

The second building to house the parochial school, illustrated on the front of the report of the committee of management for the year 1847. Several families whose names appear in this history are mentioned: Norris, Lockwood, Powell, Frampton, Pulley and Williams.
Lithograph by Goodier of Well Street, printer, after a drawing by the architect, Henry Currey
Copyright: London Metropolitan Archives

38   *A Parish in Perspective*

accepting Government money to help with school funding. Henry Currey's plans followed the same basic arrangement as the original school, with a master's house flanked by a schoolroom for the boys and a smaller one for the girls. Currey gently accentuated the consequent asymmetry by placing the bell-cote over the gable of the larger schoolroom. The new school was to be built in brick in the popular gothic style, and builder Norris was allowed nine months for the work, with a £5 penalty for every week he was late. In the event the cost turned out to be £1550. Some economies were made by re-using the fittings of the old school in the girls' new school room. The new school was opened on the day the new church was consecrated, when a supper was provided for the children and their parents in the new building.[32]

An interesting development was that the girls were now helping to raise funds for the school at the same time as practising their needlework skills. The school offered to take in cut-out work for the girls to complete according to patterns supplied by the customer. The educational value of sewing up ready-cut garments must be questioned, and it would not have taken much of this sort of work to bore the girls; perhaps leaning to endure boredom was as appropriate a preparation for their working life as any more stimulating activity. In 1847, sample prices for this work included:

fine, trimmed shirt	2/- - 2/6
common shirt	9d - 1/6
frock	6d - 3/-
pocket handkerchiefs, per dozen	9d - 1/6
night cap	3d - 6d

In 1840, Norris set up a separate school for infants in temporary accommodation in Well Street. This school moved to Ada Street in 1847 where it became the nucleus for the new parish of St Michael and All Angels, which was carved out of South Hackney in 1865.

Yet Another New Building: Monger Almshouse

Norris had an unbounded appetite for building work in the 1840s; perhaps he was conscious of creating a tangible legacy to complement the ideological one he knew he must soon be leaving. His final building project was to replace the 120-year-old Monger almshouse at the northern end of Grove Street.

In June 1848, as the church was nearing completion, the Rector and the other Monger trustees reached an agreement with George Wales for him to design and build a replacement for the old almshouse.[33] Wales was surveyor to the Cass charity, which owned land in South Hackney; a busy and efficient contractor, he had an irascible side which, as we shall see, he was to show the Monger trustees. Wales agreed to build to the same standard as the seven houses recently built to replace Joanna Martin's old wooden cottages on the land to the west of the almshouse, and to use new materials except where bricks or timber salvaged from the old building were as good as new. It was to cost £1100, part of which the trustees funded by assigning to Wales the £14 ground rent of the seven neighbouring houses for a period of fifteen years.

The agreement had not been as detailed as it could have been, and as a result there were soon misunderstandings between the parties. Wales complained to Norris that the trustees owed him £20, which they were unwilling to pay. According to Wales's later account, the Rector merely told him that the charity was 'very poor', and the trustees passed a resolution to thank Wales for 'the liberal, satisfactory and business-like manner in which he has carried out to the end and completed the whole of the transaction with them in the rebuilding of Monger's Almshouse in Grove Street, South Hackney.' Unsurprisingly, Wales regarded this 'flattering resolution' as 'an easy way of dismissing the affair' – which is probably what Norris intended it to do.

If so, he failed, though this was not clear until after his death in 1850. Goaded by further disagreements with the trustees, Wales wrote a splendidly furious letter to them in June 1851.[34] After referring to the original disagreement and Norris's reply, and detailing the current state of their financial dealings as he saw them, Wales asked the trustees, 'Can you be surprised that I should feel aggrieved? Can you be surprised that I should decline to do anything further on the present state of the matter in reference to the almshouses? My conscience acquits me that I did my duty to you. I certainly feel a pride in having been the means of helping carry out as architect and contractor a work of benevolence and although I am £100 poorer by the Building besides my loss of time still that fact would not annoy me if I had received kind and honourable treatment from the body of Monger's Trustees. ... I have done, and will never say more publicly on the subject and I should not have troubled you with these lines if I did not feel that my character might suffer imputations. I have spoken plainly and as I think every honest man has a right in this free country to assert his rights and to express his opinions when he considers he has been wronged.'

But the work had by then been done. Wales produced a most attractive design for the facade of the new almshouse based on the design of the original building, with a Dutch-style gable over a small oriel window in the

The Monger Almshouse as rebuilt by George Wales for Norris in 1847. The chimneys were removed in the 1960s and the six houses converted into four flats in 1997.
Postcard of about 1905
Courtesy of Dr Melvyn Brooks

centre and miniature turrets to articulate the ends. Stone accents including an inscribed panel in the decorative gable relieved the yellow stock brick used for the building. The facilities provided were essentially the same as those in the demolished almshouse: two rooms for each of the six almsmen, with a privy at the back.

The End of an Era

With the completion of the new almshouse in 1849, Norris's contribution to South Hackney was almost at an end. However, there remained one challenge to be confronted. Various events during the closing years of Norris's life would have worried the old Rector and landowner. The great Chartist demonstration at Kennington took place in 1848, and a series of revolutions on the European mainland followed soon after. The established order felt threatened, the Church of England included.

The Oxford Movement had split in 1845, with some of its leaders becoming Roman Catholics and others staying within the Church of England. The conversions naturally gave great encouragement to English Catholics and to the Vatican, and in October 1850 the pope appointed Nicholas Wiseman to be the first Archbishop of Westminster. As he prepared to leave Rome, Wiseman sent ahead of him a letter addressed to English Catholics which when published excited an angry response from many people in Britain who regarded it as insolent and ostentatious. Norris was naturally among them, and equally naturally he supported efforts to combat what he saw as 'popish aggression'. A petition[35] was prepared in which residents of South Hackney called upon Queen Victoria 'to defend the Protestant Church and Constitution of our Country, and to maintain inviolate the purity of our Christian Faith, and the Independence of this Imperial Realm.' The petition suggested that the 'aggression' had been 'encouraged by the vain imagination, that, because a few unstable minds have been beguiled by the sophistries of the Church of Rome, therefore, the opinions of the whole English people are accessible to the same influence.' The intemperate language demonstrates the bitterness with which even those regarded as High-Churchmen viewed both Rome and, more particularly, the ex-colleagues they saw as traitors.

This was the last public act in a long life of service to the Church of England and to South Hackney. Henry Handley Norris died after a very short illness in December 1850, to be succeeded as Rector of South Hackney by one of his curates, George Lockwood. In 1853, the parish put up a memorial to their 'beloved pastor' Norris in South Hackney church. It neatly summarises what would have been his own view of his contribution. Noting that 'this church erected mainly through him is a monument to his zeal', it recalls that 'he was among the foremost to promote the designs of piety and charity especially for the education of the poor.' It goes on: 'In an age of trial, he stood unshaken, and confirmed the faith of many by unswerving fidelity to …' And here, where we might expect 'the Lord Jesus' or 'the Church of God,' or just 'his principles', the people who knew him continue without intentional irony and with complete accuracy: '… by unswerving fidelity to the Church of England.' They included on the memorial the words of Jesus that Norris himself had selected for the tympanum over the great west door of the church: 'It is I; be not afraid'; perhaps, as is the way with mottoes, this treasured saying tells us more about Norris's state of mind than he intended.

Although his son and heir did not live in the old mansion and was to sell off the family estate in Hackney as building land, the Norris name crops up again in the next part of the story of the parish. But with the death of its dynamic, wealthy and influential first Rector, South Hackney, equipped with its new church, new school and new almshouse, had entered a new era.

ADDRESS TO THE QUEEN,

FROM

THE RECTOR, CLERGY, CHURCHWARDENS, & INHABITANTS
OF SOUTH HACKNEY,

Against the Recent Measures

OF

POPISH AGGRESSION.

TO THE QUEEN'S MOST EXCELLENT MAJESTY,

The Petition of the Rector, Clergy, Churchwardens, and undersigned Inhabitants of the Parish of South Hackney,

MOST HUMBLY SHEWETH,

That we desire to approach Your Majesty, with the Assurance of our devoted Loyalty to Your Majesty's Throne, of our unfeigned Attachment to Your Royal Person, and our entire Confidence in Your Majesty's determination to support unimpaired the Independence of the British Crown, and the Rights and Liberties of Your Majesty's Subjects.

We consider it to be our Duty, to represent to Your Majesty our Astonishment and Indignation, that in the Nineteenth Century, the Bishop of Rome should have presumed, under a pretended Divine Commission, to exercise within Your Majesty's Dominions an Authority paramount to Your Royal Sovereignty, as well as degrading to the Christian People of these Realms, and by the Nomination of a Romish Archbishop, and Bishops appointed to govern Great Britain, as a Province newly restored to the Romish See, at once to abrogate our Happy Constitution, and to introduce in its stead the most Deplorable Superstition and the most Abject Slavery.

As this aggression appears to have been encouraged by the vain imagination, that, because a few unstable minds have been beguiled by the sophistries of the Church of Rome, therefore, the opinions of the whole English People are accessible to the same influence; we rejoice in the opportunity now afforded to us, of declaring publicly before Your Majesty, that we remain unshaken in our attachment to the Protestant Religion of our Forefathers, that we cherish stedfastly in our hearts the principles of the Reformed Church, and that we continue firmly and unalterably opposed to those Errors in Doctrine and Abuses in Worship, with which successive Bishops of Rome have corrupted, and are still further corrupting, the Purity of Christianity.

We therefore most humbly implore Your Majesty to adopt such measures as Your Majesty, in Your Royal Wisdom, may consider best adapted to repel this Indignity, to defend the Protestant Church and Constitution of our Country, and to maintain inviolate the purity of our Christian Faith, and the Independence of this Imperial Realm.

And your Petitioners will ever Pray.

The Inhabitants are earnestly requested to affix their Signatures to the above Petition, which lies for Signature at Mr. SOUTHAN's *Library, Mare Street; at Mr.* STEIB's, *Mare Street; at the School-house, near Greenwood Row, Well Street; and at the house of the Beadle, Mr.* EVANS, *2, Park Cottages, near the New Church, Grove Street.*

Goodist, Printer, Hackney, and 31, Leadenhall st.

The prickly response of parts of the Church of England to Cardinal Wiseman's letter sent out of the Flaminian Gate of Rome is illustrated by South Hackney parish's Address to the Queen against Popish Aggression, 1850.
Copyright: London Metropolitan Archives

1800 to 1850: From Hamlet to Fully-fledged Parish

THE FIRST RECTOR LEAVES THE STAGE

Extract from *The English Churchman*, 19 December 1850

THE LATE REV. HENRY HANDLY NORRIS. – On Thursday last, Dec. 12, the parish of South Hackney exhibited a scene of unusual and solemn interest, at the funeral of the Rev. Henry Handly Norris, a man whose name has been for nearly the last forty years another name for the love of truth, sincerity, charity, and Christian order, – and who by his unswerving integrity and constancy in the most trying times, sustained the cause of the Church of England, and confirmed the hearts of all who wished well to her cause. His long and exemplary life, and unwearied ministerial and charitable labours, drew together a great concourse of all ranks, who vied with each other in paying a heartfelt tribute in respect of his pious memory.

He may indeed be regarded, in addition to his more public labours for the general interests of the Church, as the founder of the parish of South Hackney. Inheriting from his father a private estate, which was enough to make him independent of any learned profession, he chose the life of a Clergyman from the purest of all motives, devoting his talents in early life to a most exact study of the varied sources of sacred learning. He was the learned possessor of a store of learned theology. His residence, a handsome enclosed mansion, in the southern district of the suburban village of Hackney, was from his early years the resort of the wise and the good, who sought the advancement of the cause of sound religion and Christian education. Here, it is believed, was first planned the design of the National Society; here most of the Church's best Societies were benefited, and the cause of the Colonial Churches was fostered with untiring zeal.

But his immediate sphere of ministerial labour was around his own home. Something more than forty years since, when the interests of religion first seemed to require a Chapel of Ease to the old parochial Church of Hackney, he aided in the erection of the original Chapel of St John's, and became the Minister of it on terms highly honourable to is own generous nature. He was not one of those indolent charitable persons who are content with merely giving their alms; but, while his labour was almost or wholly gratuitous, he was always a diligent parish Priest, and refused no active service for the honour of God, or benefit of his fellow-creatures. When at length the increase of population of his district made a larger Church to be needed, though he was now a man in years, he did not rest till, by his own generous example and energetic persuasion, he had reared the present noble structure, which adorns the parish of South Hackney, at a cost, it is supposed, of a full 16,000 *l.*

His death took place on the fourth of the present month, after a very short illness, of which he had the first warning only about a week before; up to which time he had scarcely any infirmity of mind or body, though he had nearly completed his eightieth year. His last ministerial duties were in attendance on his friend, the late Bishop of Nova Scotia, and in performing the last duties at his grave.

At the funeral of the good Rector of South Hackney, the simplicity of his life was imitated in the simple arrangements made for carrying his body to the last earthly resting-place. There was no plumed hearse, or parade of hired attendants, but the coffin was born to the grave on the shoulders of such a number of bearers as are required whenever a portion of tenantless clay is to be laid with its kindred dust. The funeral-array, except a few relations and friends, was composed only of those whose feelings towards the dead brought them to the place at the appointed hour, – a large body of the London and Middlesex Clergy, and some from remote parts of the country, among whom might be observed [there follows a list of seventeen clergymen, including Challis Paroissien] and nearly all the Incumbents and Curates of the districts of Hackney and Bethnal-green. The parishioners attended in as full a congregation as is usual on a Sunday, and the large Church was crowded throughout. The service was read by Archdeacon Churton, a nephew of the deceased by marriage; and the body was laid in a vault covered by a plain flat stone near the N.E. corner of the Church which is his best monument.

This obituary for Henry Handley Norris was the main news item in this edition of *The English Churchman*. Not everyone, not even all loyal Anglicans, would have shared the obiturist's positive view of Norris. In 1833, when Norris had still been a figure of national ecclesiastical influence, Thomas Arnold might well have had him in mind when in discussing the *Principles of Church Reform* such as the shared use by Non-conformists of Anglican buildings he wrote:

But in the Church of England even bigotry often wears a softer and a nobler aspect; and there are men at once pious, high minded, intelligent, and full of all kindly feelings, whose intense love for the forms of the Church, fostered as it has been by all the best associations of their pure and holy lives, has absolutely engrossed their whole nature; they have neither eyes to see of themselves any defect in the Liturgy or Articles, nor ears to hear of such when alleged by others. It can be no ordinary church to have inspired such a devoted adoration in such men ;- nor are they ordinary men over whom the sense of high moral beauty has obtained so complete a mastery. ... But while I know the devotedness of their admiration for the Church of England, as it is now constituted, I cannot but wish that they would regard those thousands and ten thousands of their countrymen, who are excluded from its benefit; that they would consider the wrong done to our common country by these unnatural divisions among her children. *The Church of Christ* is indeed far beyond all human ties; but of all human ties, that to our country is the highest and most sacred: and *England*, to a true Englishman, ought to be dearer than the peculiar forms of The Church of England.

Chapter II

1851 to Around 1900: A Flourishing Victorian Parish

South Hackney Transformed

George Palmer Lockwood followed Norris as Rector; he had already been a curate in South Hackney for five years, and remained as Rector until his death in 1870. This was the period when South Hackney changed decisively, its remaining fields and market gardens being built over and a street layout created that has in large part survived. Most of the pre-1950 housing that survives had already been built by 1870. As Lammas land,[36] Well Street Common was spared, on account of the ancient common rights over what was still privately owned land. The new housing and the influx of residents was mixed, but not so mixed that there were extremes of wealth and poverty. Some of the streets of small working class homes that occupied the area that had been the Frampton family's park were poorly built and quickly became socially undesirable; others though small were relatively comfortable. The terraced villas, where the Grossmiths' Mr Pooter might have been at ease, were designed with moderately wealthy workers in City offices in mind, while the large houses in King Edward's Road and Victoria Park Road were built for the well-to-do City trading middle classes, with accommodation for their servants. One inevitable result of all this building was that South Hackney became for the first time a place dominated by incomers; two-thirds of elderly applicants for charity in the 1880s had come to the parish as adults,[37] many of them no doubt when the parish practically doubled in population, to 15000, between 1858 and 1861.[38] Another result of the transformation of South Hackney was a golden age for St John of Jerusalem church.

A Case to Answer

After the frenetic activity of Norris' last years, the first matter the new Rector had to deal with comes as an anti-climax. In January 1851, George Williams, one of Monger's almsmen was required to appear before the Rector, Churchwardens and the parish Overseer to answer a charge of habitual drunkenness.[39] Often ignored, alcohol abuse has nevertheless for centuries been a serious social problem in England; society's response to it has varied considerably, both generally and in South Hackney in particular. The high seriousness with which the charge against Williams was handled strikes the modern reader as painfully overbearing, but repression was then coming into vogue as the preferred response to alcohol abuse; only four years later, moralists tried to limit pub opening hours – and were confronted by riots in Hyde Park.

Before the trustees met, they had asked for Counsel's opinion as to whether they were entitled to eject the unfortunate Williams. No doubt an habitually drunken neighbour would have irritated the other almsmen, but this seemed not to be the point at issue. The barrister, a Mr Kenyon, referred to Monger's requirement for almsmen to be 'civil', saying, 'I consider the world "civil" here used to mean not only the maintenance of Good Manners but habitual propriety and decency in conduct in conformity with the rules of religion and morality and obedience to the laws of the land ... Habitual Drunkenness is, I am of the opinion, quite opposed to these. It is ... an outrage on decency and good manners, and consequently I am of the opinion that an almsman who is an habitual drunkard violates the condition on which he was admitted.' Had he been able to read this opinion, its vehemence would perhaps have surprised Williams, with his roots in the alcohol-tolerant eighteenth century, but times were changing.

Williams however was in no position to resist. He appeared and was charged and given the opportunity to explain himself. He pleaded guilty and threw himself on the 'consideration, kindness and mercy of the Meeting, with promises of future amendment.' Swayed by these pleas, the trustees confined their punishment to reproof and admonition by the rector, and Williams having 'again expressed his contriteness and renewed his promises of amendment' was allowed to return to his almshouse with the warning that he would be expelled if he re-offended. We do not know whether he did or not. Perhaps Williams's career in the East India Company had left him generally unsuited for the restrained life expected of an almsman: the Census later in 1851 found his sister-in-law living with him. It is fair to note that this may have been as much a matter of charity as of love, for there was as yet no parish almshouse for elderly women.

A New Almshouse

Such was the regard in which Henry Handley Norris had been held by many in the Church of England that within a few weeks of his death the considerable sum of £666 had been subscribed for a permanent memorial to him in South Hackney.[40] The donors included the children of the parochial school and local builder William Norris as well as parishioners, and bishops and other clergymen. Norris's widow Catherine gave £300. The question of what form the memorial might take was eventually settled in favour of a second

The original Norris almshouse erected, according to the plaque on the gable, 'in testimony of grateful affection to their late Rector, the Reverend Henry Handley Norris MA by the parishioners' in 1852. Photo taken shortly before demolition in 1967
Copyright: Hackney Archives Department

almshouse for the parish. It was to be for women, since it was understood that Norris had long regretted the restriction of Monger House to men. A trustee body legally independent of the trustees of the other parochial charities was established to build and manage the new almshouse.

Edward Hakewill, the architect of the church, was asked to prepare a design, which he submitted in June 1852. He opted once again to build in stone in the gothic style of the fourteenth century. His design, he said, made 'no other attempt at decoration than follows from good proportion and grouping of the parts and the use of proper materials.' Backward looking in style and materials, Hakewill's plan was nevertheless innovative; instead of the usual terrace of separate small houses, he proposed a single large house with five bedrooms upstairs and five individual day rooms on the ground floor, with a shared staircase, corridors, dining room and scullery. He argued that 'it has been found that the plan of solitary life usually produces a peevish and irritable temper, while the reverse is the case with the more social life which such a plan as this enables.'[41]

Whether or not Hakewill's social psychology was correct, the moment for plain, stone-built, imitative gothic had gone; the fashion was now for the creative reinterpretation of gothic in ornate brickwork. The trustees of the new fund may also have felt they had reason to distrust Hakewill's £700 estimate of the cost. So they were not beguiled by the delightful tinted perspective drawing which Hakewill submitted, and opted instead for a more conventional almshouse of only four units, designed by Charles Parker and built in brick. It cost them £1030, perhaps confirming any suspicions they may have had about Hakewill's ability to give reliable estimates. The site in Victoria Park Road was donated by Norris's son Henry, who was by now selling off the Norris estate in Hackney from his Oxfordshire home.

Clerical Strife

It cannot have been easy to follow Norris. Yet nor, surely, should it have been impossible for Lockwood to avoid some of the barely veiled reprimands that were addressed to him by Bishop Blomfield in the early months of his rectorship. Already in February 1851, the bishop was concerned that Lockwood intended without permission to 'remove the Pulpit and Desk from the present position to a spot in front of the Communion Table', making the pulpit the centre of attention, as in Non-conformist chapels; this the bishop refused to allow. The pulpit having in fact already been moved to the middle

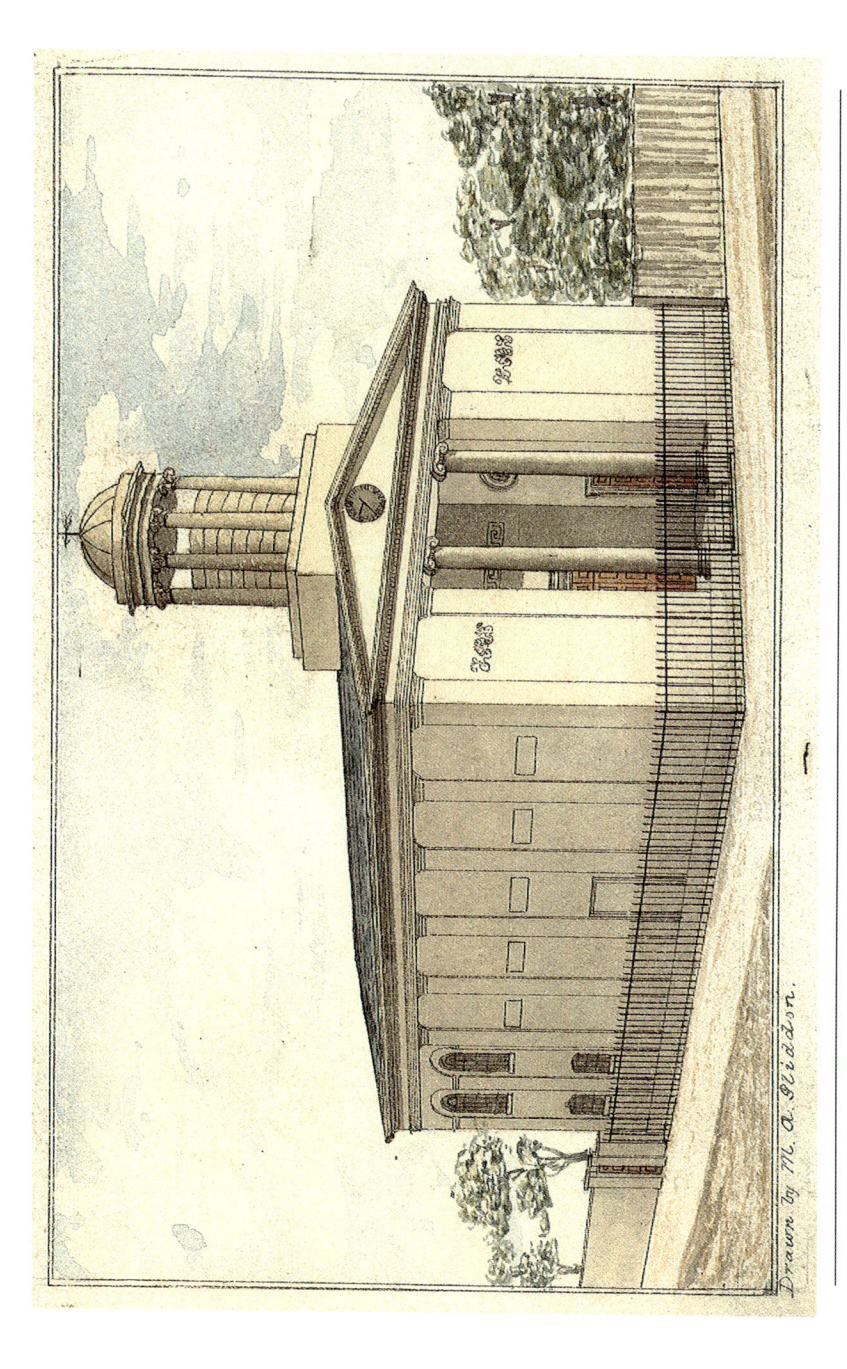

Plate 1: 'An extremely plain building.' The first St John of Jerusalem Church in South Hackney, in Well Street, built in 1810 and demolished in 1848   Watercolour by M A Gliddon, about 1830   Copyright: Hackney Archives Department

Plate 2: The portrait of the Rev Henry Handley Norris MA by Thomas Phillips, RA, presented by the parishioners in 1840
Photograph by Christine Boyd   Copyright: Christine Boyd

Plate 3: The memorial tablet to Mother Alice Bannister, moved to St John of Jerusalem church when All Saints House was demolished in 1934. The ceramic panel shows Mary presenting Jesus at the Temple, and Simeon rejoicing that he has seen 'a light to lighten the gentiles' before his death.
Photograph by Christine Boyd   Copyright: Christine Boyd

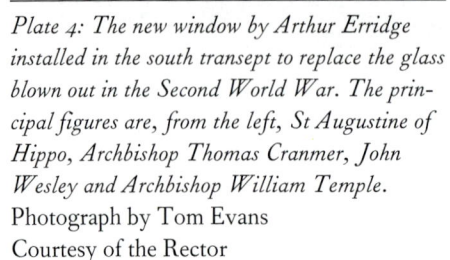

Plate 4: The new window by Arthur Erridge installed in the south transept to replace the glass blown out in the Second World War. The principal figures are, from the left, St Augustine of Hippo, Archbishop Thomas Cranmer, John Wesley and Archbishop William Temple.
Photograph by Tom Evans
Courtesy of the Rector

Plate 5: One of the two memorial windows in memory of Dorothy and Arthur Baker designed by Susan Ashworth and installed in 1998. Glimpses are included of the church, the almshouses and the school.
Photograph by Christine Boyd
Copyright: Christine Boyd

The interior of the Church after Rector Lockwood temporarily moved the pulpit in 1851. It is hard to say whether the publisher of this print, which was 'respectfully dedicated to the Rector', was a supporter or an opponent of the central pulpit.
Lithograph by C J Greenwood
Courtesy of Dr Melvyn Brooks

1851 to around 1900: A Flourishing Victorian Parish   51

of the chancel step, as shown in a contemporary engraving,[42] it now had to be moved back. Meanwhile, Lockwood was planning to abandon Norris's practice of wearing a surplice when preaching at some services. The bishop did not have strong views about this, but urged Lockwood to take notice of his congregation's wishes, and if he felt he must make the change to explain clearly that no criticism of his 'excellent predecessor' was implied. A month later, the bishop was again writing to the headstrong rector, this time about his decision to cease using the Prayer for the Church Militant, overturning the practice of previous years. It was a year before Blomfield had to write yet again, this time telling Lockwood that he could see 'no good reason' for the changes he had made in the old churchyard in Well Street.[43]

Presumably a parishioner had been complaining to the bishop about all these changes, and it is tempting to think that they represent only the efforts of a new appointee to escape the shadow of a larger-than-life predecessor, but more was involved. The Church of England was entering a period when the ritual element of its services became a topic of national interest and a cause of division in the church; Acts of Parliament were enacted on the subject, and clergymen faced prison for using rituals that by the end of the century were widespread, such as having lit candles on the altar in broad daylight. Lockwood apparently shared the fears of many that allowing such extravagant rituals in the Church of England represented a drift towards the practices and beliefs of the Roman Catholic Church; his own preferred tendency was clearly in the opposite direction, towards the practices if not the theology or politics of Non-conformists. Perhaps this was not unconnected with the fact that Lockwood had links with Anglicans in Ireland, whose church had to hold its own against generally held Catholicism; a richly carved ceremonial chair in the church commemorates his daughter's marriage to a County Fermanagh landowner.

Similar concerns surfaced again a decade later when, in 1861, Dr Williams of Pembroke Lodge in Tudor Road attempted to get a new church built in the western part of South Hackney parish. Lockwood was agitated about this, warning Bishop Tait that a minister might well be appointed who was 'notoriously infected with the Romanising error', which would introduce 'strife where all is peace and I believe would do serious mischief to the Church and to Religion.' Dr Williams claimed that he had 'no party objects and no ulterior views other than that of rendering the influence of the Church deeper and more felt in the neighbourhood with which I have been connected for more than forty years.'[44] Williams' proposal came to fruition a few years later, with the creation of two new parishes in the west of South Hackney.

The Daughter Parishes

The process of parish sub-division that had begun in Hackney in 1824 continued as the population rose. Between 1865 and 1893, parts of South Hackney parish were hived off to form the new parishes of St Michael and All Angels London Fields, St Stephen Haggerston, St Augustine of Canterbury Victoria Park, St Luke Homerton, St Mary of Eton Hackney Wick and Christ Church Gore Road. Each of these was supplied with clergy and church buildings. These parishes are mostly outside our scope, since they have retained their independent existence. However, since part of St Augustine's parish and practically the whole of Christ Church parish were later re-combined with St

The intimate but elaborate interior of Christ Church, Gore Road, built in 1871 and demolished after bomb damage in the Second World War. Photograph taken in 1920 © Crown Copyright NMR

John of Jerusalem parish – whose official name includes 'with Christ Church' – something must be said about them.

St Augustine's parish was created in 1867, taking the eastern portion of South Hackney parish towards Hackney Wick; the parish of St Mary of Eton was in turn partitioned out of St Augustine's. The South Hackney clergy had been holding services for this deprived area in temporary accommodation since about 1854. Its church was designed by J H Hakewill, brother of the architect responsible for the mother church. Unfortunately, few details of it have survived, but a photograph shows that it was a very different building from St John of Jerusalem, brick-built and with a squat, four-square tower. Evening services seem to have been the most popular at St Augustine's; in the 1880s, it was claimed that about four hundred people attended. The church was, surprisingly, built inside Victoria Park, near the Molesworth Gate; damaged by bombing in 1944 and demolished in 1957, its site is now marked only by a pattern of trees.

Lying between London Fields and St John of Jerusalem church, Christ Church parish was carved out of South Hackney in 1869. At seven thousand, its population was considerably less than that of the parent parish and the church was naturally smaller, with seats for only seven hundred. The church was consecrated in July 1871, and stood on the east side of Gore Road near its junction with Victoria Park Road,[45] where Christchurch Square now stands. As was considered proper for what was a fairly wealthy part of South Hackney, the church was rather more elaborate than St Augustine's. A tall building of eight bays with an apsidal chancel, it was designed by William Wigginton in a version of brick-built Victorian gothic with plain stone facings; there was little attempt at external ornamentation, though the interior was more elaborate and showed the impact of the Oxford Movement, for example in having a rood screen. Wigginton seems to have been somewhat cavalier in his approach to this commission, for not only did his on-site deviations from the agreed plans lose the church part of its grant from the Church Building Society, but a major outbreak of dry rot had to be dealt with within three years of the church's completion.[46]

Alterations to the Fabric of St John of Jerusalem

The *Illustrated London News* engraving of St John of Jerusalem church interior in 1848 shows no lighting equipment. A later lithograph shows two large and unattractive chandeliers hanging low over the nave; they appear to

The chancel of St John of Jerusalem church in the 1880s, showing various additions authorised since the church was built, including the subsequently removed low wall on the chancel step. The arcade walls are painted a warm red.
Copyright: London Metropolitan Archives

be oil lamps but perhaps gas was used, for Thomas Robinson, 'one of the founders and an original director of the Independent Gas Company', was buried close to the Norrises in 1852.

In 1873, two years after the appointment as rector of Ridley Daniel Tyssen, a member of the Tyssen family who were the patrons of the living, permission was obtained for a number of alterations to the church.[47] Some were never carried out, like the external door into the south transept; others, like the low stone wall across the chancel step have been reversed; and others again are still with us, notably the screen across the south transept which then provided a vestry for the choir. The pews removed to make way for the new vestry were re-fashioned to make stalls adequate for a choir of up to fifty-four men and boys. At the same time, the organ was moved out of the south transept to be closer to the choir.

Tyssen's successor, John Lester, launched another round of alterations in 1888, some of which involved reversing alterations carried out by his predecessor.[48] The organ was to be moved again, this time to a new organ loft to be built over the vestry on the north side of the chancel, and the south transept was to be opened to the congregation again; neither of these alterations was carried out. However, the inner lobby at the west end was built; until then, only an open screen stood between the main door and the nave, which must consequently have been draughty.

Both Tyssen's and Lester's programmes of alterations were approved quite early in their rectorships; they seemed to feel a need to make physical changes to the church to impose their presence on South Hackney. So perhaps it is not too surprising that Lester's successor, Vivian Lennard, who arrived in 1890, also left his mark on the church. The black-and-white floor bears the date 1893. It was probably at this time that the font was moved from its original central position just inside the screen at the west end to the west end of the north aisle.

Joseph Dodd, who followed Lennard in 1897, had few options in the matter of work on the fabric. The church was only fifty years old but a number of structural problems could not be overlooked. Damp had penetrated, or risen within, the walls, badly disfiguring the stencil work on the interior; the necessary replastering meant that some of the original decoration of the church was lost. Then there was the spire, which poor quality stone and atmospheric pollution had combined to make unsafe. In 1883, the patron and Henry Norris helped to pay for the replacement of crumbling stone and the application of fluid that was supposed to prevent corrosion, but by 1901 further repairs were urgently needed. They cost £268, almost twice the esti-

ST. JOHN'S, SOUTH HACKNEY.

The view of St John of Jerusalem church from King Edward's Road, before the plane trees in the churchyard reached their full height. The stone spire is still in place but the figures and gargoyles have already been removed because of damage caused by air pollution.
Postcard of about 1905   Courtesy of Dr Melvyn Brooks

mate, and a three-day fete and bazaar had to be held in the Rectory garden to pay for them.[49] It was at this time that the statues of the four evangelists were removed from their niches above the broaches on the spire. The same fate befell the large gargoyles of the beasts associated with the evangelists with which Hakewill had accented the corners where the tower met the spire.

1851 to around 1900: A Flourishing Victorian Parish   57

LESSONS FROM THE GRAVEYARD

The destruction in 1965 of many of the gravestones in the churchyard left only about sixty of them in place. Most of these give merely names and dates, together with a pious quotation from the bible. A few of them however are more informative and shed interesting sidelights on life in South Hackney in the nineteenth century.

Death was an all-too-familiar visitor. Frequently it was children who died. For example, George and Charlotte Anne Matthey buried two sons under four years old within three months in 1859, and an eleven year old daughter seven years later. Those who survived childhood could not count on living to a ripe old age. Charles and Mary Evans buried four children, all in their twenties or thirties. Similarly, John and Margaret Vinall lost their only child in 1873, a young man 25 years old. Divorce was not available, but the early death of partners gave many people the opportunity to marry more than once: for example, before he died aged 93 in 1903, James Thomas Tyler had buried three wives, two in the 1860s and the third, aged 56, in 1900.

South Hackney had far-flung connections even then. Samuel and Emma Matilda Hopewell came here from the small and remote south Atlantic island of St Helena; they had presumably been living there as children when Napoleon was in exile on the island. John William Crawford's home was at Golden Rock on St Kitts in the West Indies. He was almost certainly of European extraction, but it seems likely that some of little Jeanne Chang's father's ancestors were from east Asia.

The maintenance of these connections could often be dangerous work. Frederick Evans, one of Charles and Mary Evans' sons, died in 1855 at Scutari, presumably at Florence Nightingale's hospital for victims of the Crimean War, while young Hampton Michell 'perished on his homeward voyage from India, in the ship *Cleveland* supposed to have foundered with all on board in the year 1860.'

Many of the people who had moved to South Hackney were in the professional classes. Both John Vinall and James Phillips were Fellows of the Royal College of Surgeons; the latter worked at the Bethnal Green asylum for 25 years, where he 'won by his great

> kindness and skill the confidence of all.' Harriet Travis was the widow of William Travis, a member of Lloyds, while Thomas Robinson, who died in 1852 aged 72, was 'one of the founders and an original director of the Independent Gas Company'. Other activities recorded on graves include that of Charles Evans junior, who had been a 'police constable in the (A) reserve division for 15 years' before he died in 1865. Parishioners doing less-well-paid work would not have been able to afford gravestones heavy enough to resist destruction.
>
> In these years before pensions, people who survived beyond what we would think of as retirement age generally had to work as long as they could before either slipping into poverty or relying on their children. Charles Evans's grave records that when he died in 1883 aged 76, he had been for '52 years beadle of this parish'.
>
> Pleasing as it would be to know what was inscribed on the graves that were destroyed, it is likely that it would only have amplified and not changed the impression given by the surviving stones. All the fascinating information above comes from just eleven graves.

Mission Activity

In the late nineteenth century, streets of working class terraces filled the area to the north of Well Street now occupied by Frampton Park estate. On the whole their occupants showed little inclination to attend the parish church, and the clergy attempted once again to deal with this indifference by providing a separate church for them. Finding a site was not a problem: the church still owned the land in Well Street on which the original St John of Jerusalem chapel of ease had stood and which happened to be next to the target population.

It was Ridley Daniel Tyssen who in 1880 oversaw the building of St Andrew's Mission Church. The rector used his influence with his cousin and patron, the MP W A Tyssen-Amherst, later Lord Amherst, to persuade him not only to give part of the money needed for the church but also to lay its foundation stone; diaries then must have been less busy than now, since Tyssen gave his cousin only three weeks notice of the ceremony.[50] The bishop's licence maintained the fiction that the church was 'for the convenience of Inhabitants residing at a distance from the Parish Church of South Hackney', but the antiphon sung at the laying of the foundation stone came nearer the truth: 'The spirit of the Lord is upon me, because He hath anointed me to preach the gospel to the poor.' The opening of the new church was attended by the Bishop of Bedford. This was the title used until 1895 by the bishop for east London, a post then held by Bishop Walsham How, the author of some great hymns, including *For all the saints who from their labours rest*. The church was not formally consecrated but merely dedicated, which made people feel more comfortable about screening the altar off so that the rest of the building could be used for activities other than worship – though the deeds of the building forbade letting it out for money and its use for any political purpose.[51]

The building and its facilities would not have intimidated the class of people it was intended to attract. It was simply built in brick and roofed in slate, and cost less than £1300 to build and fit out; building work took less than five months.[52] There was no pipe organ until 1896, when an appeal for the necessary £38 was made to 'our richer brothers and sisters of the Parish Church'.

At first, services in the little church were calculated to appeal to the assumed level of the intended congregation: instead of matins and communion, there were mission services and children's services. As Rector Lester rather condescendingly wrote in 1888, St Andrew's was 'intended for the use of those of our poor who prefer a simple Sunday evening service, or who have not yet learned to take part in the full service of the Church.' Services were then being taken by William Harrington, one of the parish's two lay readers and a warehouse manager by trade.[53] Attendances rose when Lester's successor, Rector Lennard, made a curate responsible for the mission district; he held the normal Anglican Sunday round of matins and evensong, with regular communion services as well as children's and young men's services. By 1893, he could claim a Sunday evening attendance of two hundred. Yet even then it was said that, 'Taking the [mission] district as a whole ... the people who live in it have entirely fallen away from all practice of religion; near the parish church they are, but to it they never go. Their religion consists in sending their children to Sunday School, and attending the Watch Night service once a year.'[54]

This lack of commitment should not have surprised anyone. St Andrew's was after all a mission church, planned as a means of reaching out to people who were not church-goers. In 1896, part of this effort involved the holding of outdoor services in the streets of the mission district. How many of the

TO SEE OURSELVES AS OTHERS SEE US: WALTER SOUTHGATE

Our sources for church history in South Hackney were mostly produced by church members, so we are fortunate that a non-churchgoing parishioner recorded his outsider's view of the church's activities in Christ Church parish around 1900. Walter Southgate was born in 1890 and brought up in what is now Northiam Street, beside the Regent's Canal near where it is bridged by Cambridge Heath Road. Although just north of the Christ Church mission district, this was a desperately poor street and Southgate's autobiography *That's the Way it Was* tells a tale of working class fortitude in the face of great material deprivation.

According to Southgate, 'The cockney used the church for all ceremonious occasions such as birth, marriage and burial; otherwise he was indifferent to religious practices and left them to the educated class in society.'[55] Despite this, a certain respect was accorded to religion's outward manifestations. Although displayed beside the aspidistra on a table in the parlour-cum-bedroom, 'The Bible was purely for show, a hallmark of respectability', and 'No [street] games were allowed on Sundays.'[56] 'The clergy, as educated men from the universities, were treated by the cockney with respect and deference' – they were, after all, among the few graduates living and working in the area. But there was cynicism too: 'it was not lost upon the cockney that they bought and sold their livings like so many pork butchers who bought and sold their business.'[57]

Much of the cynicism arose from class distinction, of whose religious dimension the young Southgate was powerfully aware. Middle class church goers 'passed through North Street in their high hats, frock coats and their womenfolk overdressed in fine clothes. A working man hobnobbing with the gentry was unthinkable.'[58] This suggests that the logic of creating mission churches was correct. Pew renting in the parish church was resented as a commercial transaction in which the working class could have no part, even had they desired one: 'The front row pews or selected seats were bought and sold for a fee and an appropriate label attached to the seat.'[59]

Still, some of the church's social efforts to help the working class were seen in a positive light, even if it was felt that they had only limited impact. 'The social work of the church, judged in relation to the distress and poverty around it, was inevitably limited and touched only the fringe of a great problem. It largely consisted of soup kitchens.'[60] 'Soup kitchens were a real and necessary part of our East End life. They were a charitable effort on the part of the religious bodies for the down and outs of the area. Even the rest of the East End community were not slow to avail themselves of the cheap soup sold in these halls and hired shops.'[61]

Working class alcohol misuse was tackled by Christ Church through the Band of Hope, of which Southgate was a member. 'At the age of 10, I had signed the pledge of total abstinence from alcoholic liquor and was made a captain and given a blue sash to signify my office to take charge of other youthful abstainers from alcohol. ... [Band of Hope social] gatherings were held in a mission hall run by the Church of England at the end of our street. They were quite popular.' The Band of Hope offered other attractions, such as the annual outing to Epping Forest: 'This annual treat, the only outing in the year when, as a child, I was able to se the open country, was given to us free by the church people to all total abstainers under 12 years old. We had a long ride in four-horse brakes, a free tea of bread and strawberry jam and dollops of seedy fruit cakes.' Looking back, Southgate appreciated more than just the treats: 'The church effort was a valuable one because it got the children young enough to learn about the evils of overindulgence in alcohol.'[62]

He could see less of value in The Boys' Brigade, which 'was nothing more than dressing up in army-type uniforms, drilling, marching and carrying wooden rifles, blowing bugles, banging drums or organising drum and fife bands. This endeavour by the church to recruit youngsters into semi-military organisations caught on for a time with those in our street and the surrounding area. We all flocked to join, including myself. But the enthusiasm was shortlived.' Southgate was present at the opening night of the Christ Church Brigade, and it seems not to have gone according to plan. 'The local mission hall was crowded with boys ... Unfortunately there was not enough equipment to go round, which caused a great deal of dissatisfaction. The upshot of the opening night was that every boy disregarded orders and words of command. They formed themselves into groups and marched round the hall singing all the popular music hall ditties with appropriate cockney wording and ribald phrasing unbecoming for a church hall. ... This was hardly what the missionaries had in mind.'[63]

Overall, Southgate felt that, 'The churches had long lost their initiative and influence, if they ever possessed any among the mass of cockneys. Their approach to the problem of excessive drinking and the use of the public house was fundamentally wrong. Where the clergy were mistaken, recruited as it was from the leisured class, was its approach to most forms of public entertainment, Sunday sport and amusement – music halls as the work of the devil, a perverted view that drinking alcohol was the cause of poverty. It ignored the economic factor that, if all men kept sober, there would still be 10 men competing for five jobs in a capitalist society. The established Church missed out the cardinal factor that what the cockney craved in his drab and miserable surroundings was entertainment and decent housing. All the church was offering was church services, choirs, praying and much ritual.'[64]

Southgate's conviction that material security and comfort were needed before people could escape alcohol and begin to enjoy richer pleasures led him into politics. He became a member of the Labour Representation Committee, which went on to found the Labour Party.

target audience attended we do not know; all the church magazine records is that the services had 'never once been interrupted by an insult or a bad word from any of the bystanders.' The social investigator Charles Booth visited South Hackney church in the 1890s and noted that, 'the working class come very little either to the church or to the special mission services, and it may be doubted whether the results of this latter part of the work are commensurate with the efforts put forth.' He offered a convincing explanation for this lack of interest: 'At bottom … it is a moral obstacle with which we are confronted. What the classes above seek in religion is its support, what the working man fights shy of is its discipline. Working men have a far more exacting conception of its ethical obligations. They expect a religious man to make his life square with his opinions. … They are unwilling to accept a restraint that would deprive them of [their] everyday pleasures, and the step to denounce as hypocrites those members of religious bodies who lead mundane lives is easily made.'[65] They might, for example, have seen a contradiction in the Rector of South Hackney living in a Rectory with separate purpose-built beer and wine cellars[66] while his church promoted abstinence among the working people.

Like the mother parish, Christ Church had a mission church serving the less salubrious part of its parish, down by the Regent's Canal. All Saints mission stood at the corner of Mowlem Street and Vyner Street in what is now the London Borough of Tower Hamlets, and its buildings were described as 'probably the best of their sort in East London'.[67] Among the seriously deprived people living in this part of the parish in the 1890s was Walter Southgate, the Labour Party activist whose autobiography *That's the Way it Was* provides an insight into working class attitudes to the church.

Services at St John of Jerusalem[68]

Few records of church services have survived from the early years of this period, but Lockwood reported to the Bishop that a congregation of about a thousand filled the church most Sundays around 1860,[69] vindicating Norris's ambition in building so amply. Of this large congregation only about 100 regularly took communion.

A poster advertising the Lent services for 1853 has survived,[70] bearing witness to the enormous significance that was attached to this penitential season running up to Good Friday and Easter. A variety of clergy from north and east London gave lectures each Wednesday and practically every day during

Parish Church of South Hackney
LENT 1853.

THE FOLLOWING SERVICES WILL TAKE PLACE, (D.V.),
In the above Church, during the ensuing Season.

Ash Wednesday.

Morning Prayer at Half-past Eight. Litany, Commination Office, &c. at Eleven. Evening Service at Seven.

LECTURES WILL BE DELIVERED BY THE FOLLOWING CLERGYMEN:

Ash Wed. Feb. 9	Rev. T. TATE, M.A., Vicar of Edmonton
Wed. February 16	Rev. A. McCAUL, D.D., Rector of St. Magnus the Martyr
Wed. February 23	Rev. W. J. HALL, M.A. Vicar of Tottenham
Wed. March - 2	Rev. W. S. FINCH, M.A., Curate of West Hackney
Wed. March - 9	Rev. D. WILSON, M.A., Vicar of Islington
Wed. March - 16	Rev. J. E. COX, M.A., F.S.A., Vicar of St. Helen's

DIVINE SERVICE WILL COMMENCE AT SEVEN O'CLOCK, P.M.

During LENT, there will be Prayers every Day at Half-past Eight A.M., excepting on Wednesdays and Fridays, when they will commence at Eleven A.M.

Passion Week.

Divine Service every Day at Half-past Eight, Eleven, and Seven o'clock, (except on Good Friday). Wednesday Morning, Litany and Communion---Service at Eleven.

IN THIS WEEK LECTURES WILL BE DELIVERED AS FOLLOW:

Mon. March 21	Rev. F. R. JONES, M.A., Rector of Limehouse
Tues. March 22	Rev. T. LLOYD, M.A., Minister of St. Peter's
Wed. March 23	Rev. H. BEATTIE, M.A., Head-Master of the Orphan Asylum
Thur. March 24	Rev. T. GRIFFITH, M.A., Incumbent of Ram's Chapel

Good Friday.

Morning, at Half-past Ten . . . Rev. G. P. LOCKWOOD, M.A., Rector
Afternoon, at Three . . . . . Prayers
Evening, at Half-past Six . . . Rev. T. H. WOODROFFE, M.A., Curate
The Holy Communion at Noon.

*** On Easter Day the Holy Communion will be celebrated at Eight o'clock, A.M. as well as at the usual time.

C. J. LONDON.

Poster advertising Lent services at St John of Jerusalem church, 1853. 'DV' stands for Deo volente, *'If God is willing', piously expressing acceptance of the fact that any plan for the future may be thwarted by divine intervention; it is suggestive of Rector Lockwood's religious outlook.*
Copyright: London Metropolitan Archives

Holy Week. On Ash Wednesday, the beginning of Lent was marked by three services, one of which included the Commination Office, which has long been in disuse; its purpose was to terrify sinners into repentance by the threat of 'snares, fire and brimstone, storm and tempest; this shall be their portion to drink' unless they 'return to him, who is the merciful receiver of all true penitent sinners.' Special prayers were said daily, thrice daily in Holy Week. Four services were held on Good Friday, and there were two celebrations of Holy Communion on Easter Day.

In the 1870s, three services were being held on Sundays. Matins was said each weekday morning, and the Litany, a series of prayers covering every possible category of person in need of being prayed for, was said on Wednesdays and Fridays, as required by the Book of Common Prayer. By the end of the century, a more complex pattern of services had developed. Every Sunday, communion was celebrated at least twice, the choral celebration at noon being preceded, as it had been in the 1840s, by matins; there was a children's service in the afternoon, and evensong in the evening. Matins and evensong were said daily. The Litany was said after matins on Sundays, Wednesdays and Fridays. Baptism was available three times a week, and newly-delivered mothers could come individually for their special service of thanksgiving before or after any service. This busy schedule was maintained by the Rector and three curates; a fourth was attached to St Andrews.

Three services on Sunday and one evensong during the week were sung by the fifty-strong unpaid choir of boys and men who sat, wearing surplices,[71] in their stalls in the chancel. The only sacramental vestment worn by the clergymen was the stole;[72] at other services, we must imagine them wearing their black preaching scarves with their university hoods – usually either the black-and-white of Cambridge or the black-and-red of Oxford. The small cross which had stood for decades on the altar was felt no longer to be in keeping with the greater elaboration of services, and it was replaced in 1897 with the 'massive and beautiful' one which is still in the church, the gift, according to its Latin inscription, of 'the priests now and formerly accustomed to minister at this altar.'

The huge church was no longer full for most Sunday services. By the 1880s, it was claimed that six hundred people still regularly worshipped on Sunday mornings and 750 in the evening; twenty years later these figures had fallen to 250 and five hundred. Today's commonly held image of Victorian churches packed with worshippers is far from the truth; things have not changed as much as is often thought, in this matter at least. Rector Dodd complained in the magazine that the number of Easter communicants in 1898 was 'not so large as in former years, and not so many as ought to be gathered from a population of thirteen thousand souls.' During the 1890s, even on Easter Day, when the Church of England required all its loyal adult members to take communion, fewer than four hundred did so. This represents only about five percent of the adult population of South Hackney.

Occasional services were sometimes better attended, such as the usual midnight service on New Year's Eve in 1898, which found the church 'closely filled with an attentive congregation, very many of whom were strangers.' Another popular service was the harvest festival; in 1895 an overflowing congregation enjoyed the sight of a church decorated with flowers, fruit, bread and vegetables, along with wheat, barley and oats brought from a Norfolk farm owned by a parishioner.

Baptisms during the 1890s were running at around 300 a year, compared with 50 or so confirmations, suggesting that many more late Victorians found it important and helpful to use Anglican services as rites of passage than wished to make a specifically religious commitment. This plainly disappointed regular church-goers; even the sensible Rector Lennard, recalling how during his time in South Hackney some women who practically never came to church normally would nevertheless come to give thanks for the successful delivery of a child, commented that, 'We liked to see them come but you could hardly regard it as a religious act; it was pure superstition.'[73]

Another rite of passage was marriage, for which the new church became a popular venue. There was an eightfold rise in the number of licensed weddings in the parish, from an annual average of two in the last years of the old church building to one of 17 in Lockwood's first nine years as Rector; by the end of the century the annual figure was 120.[74] Such an increase is greater than the rise in the population of South Hackney during these years, considerable though it was. It suggests that some couples that might otherwise have married elsewhere were being married in the magnificent new church. A South Hackney wedding in July 1898 hit the headlines because a fleet of electric cars was used for the occasion, causing a sensation; as the rector presciently said, it was 'not an everyday sight, though in the future it may become common.'

Canon Lester in particular made efforts to deepen the religious convictions and understanding of his parishioners. He invited a missioner to hold a parochial mission in South Hackney in Advent 1888, and each Sunday afternoon held 'The Rector's Bible Reading', a series of 'simple Expositions of the Word of God'.

Music in the Church

When the new church was consecrated in 1848, the organ from the old church was rebuilt inside it. This old instrument, of which we have no details, was replaced in 1868. The new organ built by King seems to have been quite an impressive instrument, having three manuals, 27 speaking stops, and a pedal board that the old instrument would have lacked.[75] As enthusiasm for the church choir grew in the 1870s, the organ was moved closer to the newly-extended choir stalls, and the opportunity was taken for a rebuilding of the still new instrument, carried out by Gray and Davidson in 1873.

John Daggett, a Post Office civil servant who was organist and choirmaster in the 1880s, was clearly up-to-the-minute: his choir was singing Sir John Stainer's cantata *The Crucifixion* in 1888, the year following its publication. The rector, Canon Lester, took care to see that this was not seen merely as a concert of religious music; the cantata was sung every Wednesday evening during Lent as the centrepiece of the church's Lenten devotions.

Daggett's successor was South Hackney's most celebrated organist. John E West lived locally in King Edward Road, the son of William West who seems also to have been organist at the church. He was appointed organist and choirmaster in 1891 at the age of 27; he stayed only until 1897 but he had by then transformed the musical life of the church, whose choir was by now fifty strong. This involved a lot of hard work for all concerned, as an article by West in the September 1896 church magazine makes clear: 'Those who attend our services and appreciate the music little know, perhaps, the amount of labour that is spent week by week practising the choir. The practices for the boys are now held practically *daily* (sometimes in the evening, at other times as early as eight o'clock in the morning), taking up a great deal of the Choirmaster's time and considerably shortening the hours of recreation for the boys.' His musical ambition getting the better of his tact, West continued: 'The results at the services are, of course, remarkably successful, considering all things; but our fine Parish Church should have the *very best* choir that can be obtained from the neighbourhood. ... It is an undoubted fact that many of the boys who belong to South Hackney Church choir would never have been admitted by the Choirmaster at a church of any musical pretensions, although it is only fair to say that they are all good and willing lads, and do their very best under the circumstances.' To try to deter local boys with good voices and sight-reading ability from joining paid choirs in City churches, West arranged two choral scholarships at Parmiters School for South Hackney

Queen's College

John E West, 1897

Queen's College – *a long metre hymn tune by John E West.*
Try it to When I survey the wondrous cross

1851 to around 1900: A Flourishing Victorian Parish

choristers between 11 and 13 years of age, to be paid for by the churchwardens.

West also composed pieces for South Hackney church. By no means was all of it as frivolous and ephemeral as the music he wrote for the children's 1895 Christmas play, *My Lady Poppy, or the Sleeping Beauty*. His 1894 anthem *Now is Christ risen* was dedicated 'To the choir of South Hackney Parish Church'. The choral writing is clearly aimed at a choir whose technical abilities were quite limited, while the organ accompaniment makes no such allowance. Anthems were sung at every Sunday evensong. Often they were by West – even long after he had left the church – but other better known composers were represented, including Handel, Mendelssohn, Stainer, Wesley, Gounod and Spohr. Bach seems not to have been attempted. The choir also had several settings of the communion service in its repertoire. Queen Victoria's Jubilee in June 1897 was celebrated using Novellos' special hymn book, with words by a former South Hackney curate, W J Ferrar; the tunes included one by West.

As well as singing the choral services, West's choir also put on concerts in the church, accompanied by both organ and an orchestra. An 1895 performance of the popular *Hymn of Praise* by Mendelssohn was followed by West's own *Te Deum*; unfortunately the effort they put into this concert seems to have exhausted the singers, so few of whom turned up next morning at 7am that the planned choral service had to be replaced with a said service. It was one of the hazards of relying on volunteers.

Happily, choir life was not all hard work. There were theatre trips for the choirboys,[76] and they put on a play each Christmas, while the men enjoyed an annual dinner with the organist and clergy. But the amount of work required to obtain relatively mediocre results was one reason for West's departure. It is pleasant to know that his contribution was valued by Rector Lennard, who wrote in the church magazine of West's 'valuable and really splendid services in the past', hoping that 'his talents and enthusiasm may find a sphere of greater scope than is offered by the weekly services of an ordinary Parish Church.' After a final farewell organ recital West left, leaving one of his pupils, R Bernard Elliott, to take his place.

Elliott won the job against the stiff competition of two Fellows of the Royal College of Organists, but as well as already being the assistant organist he had the advantage of being a teacher running a school choir of 120 boys. He stayed an astonishing 37 years and did his best to maintain the musical tradition in changing times, with for example devotional performances of Stainer's *The Crucifixion* during Holy Week. Like his mentor, he composed

SOUTH HACKNEY MUSICIAN FINDS A WIDER PUBLIC: JOHN E WEST, FRCO, FRAM

Adapted with permission from the web site http://www.johnwest.org.uk by Andrew Houston, who plans to complete his Edinburgh doctoral thesis on West in the near future.

John Ebenezer William West was born on 7 December 1863 and brought up in King Edward Road, South Hackney. His father, William West, also an organist, founded the North East London Academy of Music. His mother, the self-styled Madame Clara West, was a professional soprano, and his sister, Lottie West, a contralto soloist, pianist and teacher. West was taught at home by his father and received organ lessons from Sir Frederick Bridge, organist at Westminster Abbey. From 1880 until 1882 he studied at the Royal Academy of Music where he was taught composition by his Dalston-based uncle, Ebenezer Prout, editor of Handel's *Messiah* and respected authority on the fugues of J S Bach. He gained the Associateship of the Academy in 1883 and the following year passed the Fellowship exam of what was soon to become the Royal College of Organists.

West held successive organ posts in London at St Mary's Bourdon Street (1884–1891), St John of Jerusalem South Hackney (1891–1897), and St Augustine's Queen's Gate (1897–1902). He conducted various choral societies and choirs in London, Reading, Croydon and Warlingham, and lastly the highly regarded Railway Clearing House Male Voice Choir.

In 1884, on his twenty-first birthday, West entered the music-publishing firm of Novello & Company in London as an associate editor. Following the death of Berthold Tours in 1897, West succeeded to the post of chief editor and advisor. He was following in illustrious footsteps: apart from Tours, Sir Joseph Barnby and Sir John Stainer had occupied the post. He remained at Novello's for forty-five years, of which thirty-two were spent as chief editor. In this post he would have had a considerable say as to what was published and would have had the ear of most of the leading British musicians of his day. Elgar's work was published by Novello's, and

West on several occasions returned work to him suggesting alterations and pointing out mistakes; he told Novello's board that Elgar's part-song *Zut, zut* was an inferior work. Such behaviour did not endear him to Novello's influential publications manager, August Jaeger, who was so close to Elgar that he appears as 'Nimrod' in the *Enigma Variations*.

He was a prolific composer and editor: the British Library holds over five hundred pieces of printed music by him, both original compositions and editions. His output consists mainly of sacred and secular choral compositions, original organ music, transcriptions of orchestral music for organ, and editions of choral and organ music spanning four centuries. In his day, he was well respected, as is evident from correspondence and frequent reviews in *The Musical Times*.

West's sacred choral compositions include many anthems and settings of the canticles commissioned by or dedicated to leading choirs of the day, such as those of Westminster Abbey, St Paul's and Lichfield Cathedral. Frequently performed until Victorian music fell out of fashion, they are not difficult to sing, and the organ accompaniments, though more taxing, are never allowed to dominate. The handful of establishments that now perform his music agree that it is successful because it is ably crafted and written well for the voice, and that he deserves to be sung as often as Stanford, Parry and Stainer. Indeed his cantatas can rank alongside works such as Stainer's *The Crucifixion*. He wrote many hymn tunes, some of which, such as *Queen's College* and *Blessed Saviour*, are excellent examples of this miniature form. Much the same can be said for some of the part-songs West wrote for the many madrigal societies, glee clubs and male voice choirs that were active then.

West's compositions for the organ were often dedicated to leading musicians of the day and are well worth reviving. Their bold, sweeping style bears a resemblance to Elgar's. But a great deal of his work for the organ was editorial. He edited a series of English organ music which had been written before organs with pedals were introduced to England, carefully retaining the original harmonic structure while filling out the harmony, providing a pedal part and giving suggestions as to expression, phrasing and registration. In the days before radio and cheap recordings, West helped to bring serious music to people who could not afford admission to orchestral concerts by his transcriptions of orchestral works, much of it for organ but including a version of Elgar's *Enigma Variations* for pianoforte duet.

The choral editions prepared by West include Bach's *Six Motets*, Palestrina's *Loquibantur variis linguis* and Brahms's *German Requiem*, though most of them are by English composers, from Byrd to Ouseley.

With an output of such volume, quality and variety, we have to ask why West's music is now all but forgotten.

John E West FRCO FRAM

No doubt fashion and Jaeger's enmity had something to do with it. But perhaps the main reason for his eclipse may have been of his own doing. According to his obituarist, West was a modest, unassuming man; he preferred to keep out of the limelight and instead got on with the work in hand. Once the music had been written, published and performed, he considered the job done. He appears to have had no desire to push his music or promote its performance; he seldom performed any of his own music at concerts he conducted and rarely played any of his own organ compositions, commenting once that he regarded them as 'inadequate'.

Despite this, West was awarded the Fellowship of the Royal Academy of Music in 1919 for his services to music and for bringing distinction upon his alma mater. He collapsed on the stage of the Westminster Central Hall on 28 February 1929, after conducting the third item in a concert by the Railway Clearing House Male Voice Choir. He was rushed to nearby Westminster Hospital where he was pronounced dead. He would have been driven past the twin towers of Westminster Abbey where his career had really begun fifty years before.

canticle settings and pieces for the organ, and also wrote the music for the choir boys' Christmas plays, including *Dick Whittington and his Cat*.[77] We must hope that his music was at least the equal of the lyrics, written by one of the curates, which are so artless as to demand quotation. The *Song of Soup* runs:

> *Take a load of artichokes*
> *Mix within a heap of spices*
> *Make it strong as farthing smokes*
> *Make it thick as penny ices.*
>
> Chorus:
> *Soup, soup, beautiful soup*
> *Better than Bovril, sounder than Brand.*
> *Liebig is poor to you*
> *Bovril – no more of you*
> *Soup of South Hackney,*
> *Best in the land!*

Women in the Church

At this time, girls and women were not admitted to church choirs. But around 1880, it began to be a matter of general concern in the Church of England that the proportion of women relative to men at church services was steadily rising. South Hackney bore out the trend: in the 1890s, almost three-quarters both of the confirmation candidates and of the Sunday school teachers were women.[78] This change had a profound impact on church life, in South Hackney as elsewhere.

Because in the nineteenth century women were not permitted to join the ancient orders of the ordained ministry yet wanted, and were needed, to carry out a recognised ministry in the Anglican church, orders of 'deaconesses' were founded beginning in the 1860s. Their role was principally to carry out systematic visitations to homes around the parishes to which they were attached; they had no role inside the church building except to look after the altar linen and organise church cleaning. There was no clear distinction between the deaconesses and the Anglican orders of sisters that were being founded around the same time.

In 1880, Bishop Walsham How founded a group of celibate deaconesses, the East London Deaconess Community,[79] 'to extend the primitive order of deaconesses and to train devout women for the office, [and] to help the clergy in east and north London who require the assistance of deaconesses in their respective parishes.' In 1895, the members made their headquarters in South Hackney in the house that stood where Meynell Gardens is today. Called All Saints House, it was equipped with its own chapel, served by a male chaplain, Herbert Eck. The deaconesses were integrated into the life of the parish. Walsham How 'ordained' three women and admitted them to the community in a ceremony held in St John of Jerusalem church in 1895; a further two were admitted in 1896. By 1901, the house housed four full members of the community, two associates and four women church workers, together with their three servants.[80] Bible classes for girls and young women from the church were held at All Saints House, led by Mother Alice Bannister. She was Head Deaconess from 1889 until her death in 1908, and a most attractive ceramic, mosaic and marble tablet in memory of her is in the church. Rector Lennard was clearly pleased with the connection, writing in the church magazine in May 1896 that 'Our better class girls ought to feel it a great privilege to be able to obtain religious instruction from so able and experienced a teacher. It is an opportunity which every parish does not supply.' Perhaps his experience in South Hackney lay behind his 1910 book *Woman: Her Power, Influence and Mission*. Sunday school classes were held in the House at least until the Great War, by when Sister Maud of All Saints House was being listed among the parish clergy. Christ Church Gore Road was also served by a deaconess towards the end of the century.

The Girls' Friendly Society, whose primary purpose was 'the preservation of purity' among girls, had a branch in South Hackney. The Guild of St Mary the Virgin was intended to promote 'the increase of devotion and the deepening of the spiritual life', but its members seem to have had plenty of fun, with their hilarious seaside outings being written up in the church magazine. There was a Mothers' Meeting in the parish. A dozen or so 'earnest church women' had areas allotted to them in which they hoped to 'influence for good' poor people, and to 'recommend for relief cases of real distress.' Financial help was given to poor mothers, so long as they were married, and the leisured ladies of the mother church met to sew clothes for the hard-pressed mothers of the mission district. That the church's Mothers' Meeting found it desirable in 1895 to hold talks on such matters as 'diseases that may be carried by impure water' and 'infection from drains, cisterns, sinks and dustbins' is a stark reminder of the grimly insanitary conditions endured by all too many of Queen Victoria's subjects.[81] An annual Mothers' Tea was held for mothers in the mission district; the mothers evidently rarely went to church, since the rector found it necessary to tell the 120 attenders in 1898 that coming to the Mothers' Tea 'ought to lead naturally to attendance at the Sunday services in the Mission or the Parish Church'. Perhaps rather cynically, Booth noted that the women who attended these mothers meetings were more 'inclined to hypocrisy and cadginess' than their menfolk, who generally refused to have anything to do with the church.[82]

The Men and the Boys

While women's influence grew, efforts were being made to stem the haemorrhage of men. The church had its cricket and football teams in the 1880s though the South Hackney football team, unlike others attached to parishes, did not prosper to become a member of the Football Association.

In the 1890s, the Church Lads' Brigade spread widely through the Anglican church. Like the Salvation Army, it capitalised on a late Victorian fondness for military uniforms, terminology and discipline. A branch, or 'company', was founded in South Hackney, where 'Everything is done on a military basis. ... A transition is effected before very long from the slouching, loafing, untidy fellow, to the smart soldier aspect of uprightness and attention. ... It is a sort of new crusade against all impurity, unmanliness and wrong.' Throughout the '90s, the Company numbered about fifty lads, who often paraded in uniform in church on Sundays. A comment in the magazine in March 1900 captures the flavour of these church parades: 'The drums of South Hackney Company were used with fine effect in the recessional hymn *Onward, Christian Soldiers.*'

At All Saints' mission at Cambridge Heath meanwhile, after the shaky start recorded by Southgate, the similar Boys' Brigade grew to be large enough to form 'four squads under the command of their non-commissioned officers'; they competed in rifle drill competitions, one of which in December 1901 was judged by 'Major Bartholomew, the Commanding officer of the South Hackney Battalion of the Church Lads Brigade.'

'Purity' is not a term that is often heard today, so it is striking that the Church Lads' Brigade, like the Girls' Friendly Society, placed purity at the top of its agenda. There was also a Church of England Purity Society at this time. The purity all these organisations had principally in mind was sexual purity, by which was meant the prohibition of autoerotic and homosexual activity and the absolute restriction of heterosexual activity to marriage.

The Guild of St John the Baptist offered men an opportunity to debate religious matters. Their meetings in the 1890s typically began with the reading of a paper about some topic such as the authorship of one of the New Testament epistles, its place in the New Testament and modern views as to its meaning and importance.

In the 1890s, a house in what is now Kingshold Road was taken by the church to be used as a clubhouse for young working men. It lay conveniently close to the St Andrew's mission district. Various sports including boxing and fencing were encouraged, as were games of all kinds. There was also a reading room. Regular debates about topical issues were held, at one of which in 1897 the rights and wrongs of strikes were discussed; the magazine did not shrink from reporting that 'As regards strikes, the opinion seemed to be very decidedly that they are justifiable.' Since the overall purpose of the club was 'to keep a hold on the young men, and keep them from joining clubs of a doubtful character', the club had to be open more or less the same hours as its rivals, that is, every evening – except Sunday, when it was hoped that the young men were attending St Andrew's mission church for the weekly service designed especially for them. Again, Booth offers the view from outside: 'Many churches [in Hackney generally] have organised large clubs for working men, but they have been constrained as a necessary condition to banish from them all overt ideas of religion. The men will not have it.'[83]

Other Church Activities

Apart from these sex-specific activities, the church in South Hackney in the 1890s had a full schedule of other activities. They covered the spectrum from recreational and cultural, through the social and charitable to the essentially missionary.

There were cycling and rambling groups; they needed to make it explicit that 'ladies are invited' to go on their trips to such places as Ightham Mote, Eltham and Hayes. A Literary Society met to discuss, for example, the works of George Eliot, Milton and Dickens; there were also separate ladies' and men's Shakespeare Societies at whose meetings plays were read and discussed. The parish's full string orchestra gave its sixth annual concert in 1896 under the baton of Dr Ambrose Kibbler to raise funds for the annual seaside excursion of the Mothers' Meeting, of which Mrs Kibbler was superintendent.

Booth noted that 'over a large part of Hackney, it seems to be regarded as part of the duty of the church to supply decent amusements, and entertainments in winter time are described as "incessant", consisting of dances, balls, concerts, plays, and, in two of the parishes [including South Hackney] culminating in an annual pantomime. ... Usually there are ulterior spiritual motives. But these social efforts come to have a life of their own which requires little other justification.'[84] Rector Dodd's comment about the Mothers' Meeting suggests it was unlikely that the clergy of the day would have shared his view.

The soup kitchen was a major charitable effort, making and distributing up to 300 gallons of soup each week to the poor in the St Andrew's mission district at lunchtime on Wednesdays and Fridays during the winter months. A curious aspect of the scheme was that books of tickets were sold to better-off parishioners, who could then distribute the tickets as they saw fit, perhaps directly to poor, 'deserving' individuals they knew, or through the parish clergy or district visitors; 24 tickets cost five shillings in 1888. This was not an uncommon way of funding charities; in these days long before the health service was founded, letters referring people to hospital were similarly bought in bulk by donors and distributed to the poor by the clergy. Each person presenting a soup ticket at the kitchen received a quart of soup and a small bread roll, for which they paid a halfpenny. At this rate, there must have been up to six hundred people needing a cheap, nourishing meal in a parish of about 13,000; as the magazine commented in February 1900, 'The need is great'.

In these days when the poor really were desperately poor and had little access to banking facilities and no state benefits, the parish organised various savings schemes for the less well off, including a Penny Bank and a mutual loan and saving scheme. The provident societies for the poor were particularly ingenious: donations from better-off supporters allowed such schemes to pay an annual bonus of 1d or 2d on each shilling saved, which was then paid back in the form of vouchers for clothing and coal. A Christmas Goose Club helped over two hundred poorer families save up for the expensive things that were needed to celebrate the festival:[85] as well as a goose or turkey or a joint of beef, the saved-up 6/6 paid for half-a-pound of tea, a pound of sugar, a pound of raisins, half-a-pound of currants, half-a-pound of suet and some holly, a Christmas card and a parish calendar. To modern appetites, this would hardly constitute a Christmas feast.

Alcoholism continued to be a serious social problem, with poor families commonly spending up to a quarter of their inadequate income on alcohol, and the church in South Hackney attempted to tackle it; there was a branch of the Church of England Temperance Society with 90 abstaining members, while the Band of Hope encouraged its hundred or so children to just say no under the three-fold pledge: 'No strong drink, no bad language, no untruthfulness'.

The St John of Jerusalem Sunday school was large, catering for the children not only of church-goers but also of those who were otherwise engaged on Sunday. Well over four hundred children were taught by about fifty teachers in a variety of venues, including the parochial day school and All Saints House; the St Andrew's Sunday school was about the same size. Children and teachers were expected to attend both morning and afternoon sessions on Sunday. The whole school followed the same curriculum, and the magazine published the topics for forthcoming Sundays. For these lessons, the pupils were divided by sex, as indeed they were for the parish library, which was open on Tuesday evenings 'for boys and girls alternately'. Children who attended Sunday school regularly were given an annual treat, such as their summer trip in 1913, when 220 children went by rail to Theydon Bois to visit the fair. They also enjoyed a Christmas party, with small gifts for everyone.

As Southgate records, the opportunity to get out of London, to escape if only for a short time its pollution and overcrowding, was highly valued. In the 1880s, the church ran two schemes to make country holidays possible for those who could otherwise not afford them. The parish nominated ailing children to go into the country for a fortnight or more in the summer under the auspices of the Children's Country Holiday Fund. The Rector's Country Rest Fund was a local initiative, 'intended for Communicants who are weary and worn by work and business, and are unable to procure for themselves needful rest and change. A village-parish in one of the prettiest and most healthy parts of Essex is attached to our parish for this purpose. Our visitors are received by the Vicar, and during their stay are under his pastoral care. They live as guests in suitable cottage homes, and have the privilege of the Daily Service in the Village Church.'

Relations with Other Churches

In the two South Hackney parishes of St John of Jerusalem and Christ Church, there were in the 1890s a total of fourteen places of Christian worship, including the two parish churches and their mission churches. Not a great deal can be said about ecumenical relations, for Anglicans formally had very little to do with any of the others; even exchanges of pulpits between Anglicans and Non-conformists were still forbidden. However by the end of the century, things had improved somewhat on the earlier frostiness. At a personal level, relations between Anglican ministers and other Christian clergy could be 'very friendly', and Rector Dodd told the bishop 'I have always met with the kindest treatment from ministers of other bodies.'[86]

Yet Booth observed that in Hackney generally there was 'not a little bitterness of feeling' between the Anglicans and the Non-conformists.[87] The bitterness was not all religious, for this was the heyday of non-conformist political influence, exercised through the Liberal party; it is no surprise that the only Member of Parliament known to have belonged to the St John of Jerusalem congregation was a Conservative, Herbert Robertson,[88] who represented South Hackney from 1895 until ousted by the egregious swindler Horatio Bottomley in 1906.

Clergy and Rectory

The house in Tryon's Place which had been bought as a parsonage when South Hackney church was in Well Street was not suitable to be the Rectory when the present church was built. This hardly mattered while Henry Handley Norris was Rector and lived in his nearby mansion, leaving the Tryon's Place building to be occupied by one of his curates. However, after his death, it became necessary to provide a new Rectory. The northernmost corner of Norris's park, just across the road from the church, was obtained and on it was built a large and rather ugly brick house on four floors, surrounded by a generous garden. Part of the cost was raised by the sale of the Tryon's Place house and part by borrowing from Queen Anne's Bounty, a fund set up by the Queen which continues to support the Church of England under the more prosaic name of the Church Commissioners. The remaining debt was paid off by Lord Amherst in 1885. When occupied by a married Rector with a young family, the Rectory needed four servants to run it; bachelors like Rector Dodd made do with only two.[89]

The clergy who served South Hackney in this period were uniformly male and well-educated, if only in a narrow curriculum. All the rectors and most of their curates were graduates of either Oxford or Cambridge, where they had studied such subjects as maths, law, classics and history. Most of them had led conventional clerical lives before coming to South Hackney, attending university, going on in some cases to one of the then-new theological

The enormous gothic-horror first Rectory, built at the corner of Church Crescent and Groombridge Road in the early 1870s, sold to Toc H as a hostel in 1931 and replaced by Prideaux House in 1962. Its basement included separate wine and beer cellars, and its attics accommodated four servants.
Photograph by George James, about 1873
Copyright: Hackney Archives Department

colleges, and then taking a series of curacies. Others had had less conventional careers; the group includes men with experience in school teaching, missionary work and medicine. Rector Iliff had spent most of his career as an organiser for the Church of England Temperance Society. Dr John Egan, a South Hackney curate and later vicar of Christ Church for its first twenty years, was a Glasgow-trained medical doctor who before ordination had succeeded his father as medical superintendent of a Dublin hospital for sexually-transmitted diseases. One of the curates, Ernest Rackwitz Sequira, was a local man who had attended St John of Jerusalem church before being ordained and working first as a missioner at St Paul's Bethnal Green.

For pastoral purposes, each parish was divided up between the incumbent and his several curates. It is perhaps significant that towards the end of the century, the only non-graduate clergyman of Christ Church parish was the

DIFFERENCES OF APPROACH

Despite their obvious similarities, the clergy who have served as Rectors of South Hackney have varied greatly, even in matters very closely connected to their function as priests. One way to appreciate this is to contrast their writings. Two nineteenth century Rectors were particularly prolific authors. The first Rector, Henry Handley Norris, published several sermons and polemical tracts, and his *A Parson's Legacy* was prepared posthumously from his papers; he is also understood to have been the author of the anonymous *A Manual for the Parish Priest, Being a Few Hints on Pastoral Care to the Younger Clergy of the Church of England; From an Elder Brother*. The *Manual* was published in 1815 and was popular enough to have been reprinted in 1822. Vivian Lennard published several collections of sermons, some of which may date from his time in South Hackney in the 1890s; the collections include *Woman: Her Power, Influence and Mission*, of 1910. Norris and Lennard were men of very different temper, as is shown by these extracts dealing with the care of young people and those in distress.

Young People

At the age for confirmation, young persons are just entering the most important and dangerous period of their lives. In the height of youthful ardor, they are going to encounter the temptations of the world. … Let the careful pastor by no means lose the opportunity now afforded him of urging upon this part of his flock the necessity of the greatest consideration and watchfulness, to press upon them the observance of religious duties, and carefully to avoid the company of the dissolute and the haunts of intemperance.

From Norris's Manual, *Chapter One: 'The Public Duties of the Parochial Clergy', page 80*

For of one thing I am certain, that many a religious home is really a bad school in this respect, that it fails to encourage independence. Its teaching and ideals are so narrow and restricted that ... the wider world that lies beyond immediately encourages a revolt against the thoughts and maxims of home, and the boy brought up in strict Evangelical or extreme High-Church views, is destined to receive such rude shocks to his faith as may seriously threaten his belief in God altogether. ... It is, I say, a terrible thing to make the inevitable independence of the man (which must come sooner or later), a thing which is forced upon him by the violence of a sudden wrench, and the bitterness of a great reaction.

From Lennard's sermon 'First Steps', in Woman, *page 67*

Those in Distress

When such an opportunity occurs of awakening to a sense of his duty the transgressor of God's laws or rousing the attention of a careless Christian, it should not be allowed to pass by; returning health may harden a heart softened only by sickness. ... This is the time for him who is set to watch for the souls of his parishioners to discourse both upon the terrors and upon the mercies of the Lord, to use every method to persuade the nominal Christian to become a real Christian.

On visiting the sick, from Norris's Manual, *Chapter Two: 'The Private Labours of the Parochial Clergy', pages 88 & 91*

You cannot enter a house where grief has not entered before you. ... Beneath the smiling mask which Society wears there lurks many a hidden sorrow which is eating the heart out, many a suffering soul that is weeping in private and praying for a little sympathy. We know nothing of the gloom and ennui, the bitterness and despair which are rankling in the bosoms of those whom we meet with day by day in the great thoroughfares of life.

From Lennard's sermon 'The Discipline of Sorrow', in Woman, *page 148* one given responsibility for the Cambridge Heath mission district; the Rector of St John of Jerusalem meanwhile undertook pastoral work in a few of the most prosperous middle class roads in the parish, which happened to be round the corner from the Rectory. One of the South Hackney curates was usually made chaplain to the residents of the French Protestant Hospital – that is, elderly people's home – that was built in 1866 on land where a few thatched cottages had stood in Norris's time.

The rectors in particular were often well-connected. As we have seen, Daniel Tyssen was a member of the family of the patron, while Rector Lennard spent part of one of his holidays saying services for the Earl and Countess of Ancaster at Drummond Castle, near Crieff in Scotland.

Several of the South Hackney clergy published books, though not usually while they were serving the parish; perhaps this busy urban parish allowed insufficient time for writing. Their books were often collections of sermons, like Rector Lockwood's *Sermons on the Antiquity of Church Liturgy*[90] and Rector Lennard's book on women's ministry. W J Ferrar, who was a curate during the 1890s, published many collections of poetry as well as theological works. Vicar Egan's book on syphilitic diseases, written in 1853 before his ordination, described how he had introduced the use of the speculum into the UK and opposed treatment with mercury; his book is notable for its admirably non-judgemental approach to those suffering with these diseases.

Illuminating as it is, such information tells us little about what these men were like. Occasionally however their public writings give us a hint of personality. Vivian Lennard, for example, announcing his departure from South Hackney Rectory in August 1897, wrote a paragraph which could be written only by someone of genuine warmth and sensitivity: 'Partings all seem to come too suddenly at last, and I know our regrets will deepen as the time draws near. The links which bind a clergyman to his people are multiplied and strengthened as the years roll on. They have their root in the tenderest associations and most solemn experiences of our lives. The memory of the dead passes into them. For the most ordinary offices of our sacred calling are inseparably connected with the greatest epochs in human life. It is always so with a clergyman. His duties bring him into daily contact with the lives of others, and the influence cannot but be felt on both sides.'

Resources

Five clergymen, two churches, a school and all these church activities absorbed considerable resources, the most obvious of which was money. One popular early nineteenth century fundraising activity, the preaching of charity sermons, had already fallen into disuse by the 1860s. We have seen how appeals, usually with lists of subscribers and their donations, garden fetes and the sale of charity tickets were employed in the search for money; these too have now disappeared. Other methods remain common today, including bazaars and 'American sales' – by which was meant jumble sales. Such events require a lot of work from their organisers, and appropriate gratitude was sometimes shown; a Mr Hensler was given a silver inkstand in June 1902 'in recognition of his services as secretary of the South Hackney Church Bazaar.' Then there were the Sunday collections. In order to put a little psychological pressure on those 'many who come occasionally [and] give nothing' at the collection, it was decided in 1895 to pass round open alms-dishes at evening service, in the hope that 'alms-dishes may appeal more forcibly than the bags which are at present in use.'

Some of the church's nineteenth-century fund-raising methods are less familiar today. From medieval times until 1868, the local Anglican church was empowered to levy a tax, called the church rate, on all householders whether or not they were Anglican or even Christian. Unpopular as it was with non-conformists, this had made some sense so long as the church was practically the local authority, but when new, accountable and secular local authorities were created in the 1850s, it was rapidly seen that the ancient system was no longer tenable. In South Hackney, a meeting of ratepayers in August 1856 rejected the proposed church rate of 4d in the pound. Interestingly, the proposal was then immediately put to a referendum of all ratepayers in the parish, who rejected it by 371 votes to 203.[91] To his credit, and unlike his counterparts elsewhere in Hackney, Rector Lockwood seems to have recognised that times had changed. He continued to set a church rate but in practice payment was voluntary, and much unpleasantness was thereby avoided.

Another unfamiliar approach to fundraising was pew renting, which provided much of the money to pay the clergy. Even today the pews in the church bear traces of numbers and nameplates which were used to identify which pews had been rented by whom. When the church was new, the total income from rented pews was the considerable sum of £460.10.0 a year, raised from rents which ranged from £1.10.0 for the best seats down to five shillings. Henry Handley Norris rented ten of the most expensive seats for his family and another six at five shillings for his servants.[92] Both the number and the cost of these 'sittings', as they were called, fell during the later nineteenth century; over half the places were rented in 1872, but only about a quarter by the 1890s, by which time the incomes from sittings had fallen to around £230. It seems that renting a pew was seen to be less of a social imperative as the period drew to a close.

It is easy to misunderstand the pew renting system, especially when we think of the free benches in the central aisle; it can easily seem that wealthy and often absentee pew-renters were forcing the poor church-goer to chose between a seat in a pew with a poor view and a chilly, uncomfortable bench. Rector Lennard attempted to justify the system in the June 1896 church magazine: 'It is not obvious to strangers at our Sunday services, who are freely shown to the best seats, that S John's is a pew-rented church, nor is it perhaps generally known that while nearly three-fourths of the sittings are free, the income derived from Pew Rents form a considerable part of the endowment of the living.' Differences in treatment according to one's wealth and class were in any case common at the time; at the *Hackney Empire* music hall, those in the cheaper upper gallery seats were not even allowed in through the front door and were not allowed to mix with those who were.

Most of the money came from the middle class people attending St John of Jerusalem church. In the 1890s, typical monthly collections were £30 at St John of Jerusalem and £2 at St Andrew's. These funds were to some extent pooled. The purchase of an organ for St Andrew's by the congregation of St John of Jerusalem illustrates one of the advantages of, as it were, twinning neighbouring wealthy and poor churches, an advantage which was practically lost when parishes were formally split. The congregation of the mother church not only provided funds for the daughter church but also provided most of the leadership for the social support projects in the mission area. For as well as being wealthier than the people of the mission district, the 'richer brothers and sisters of the Parish Church'[93] enjoyed greater leisure, a better education and useful connections. All these were required to support the wide range of church activities we have reviewed.

The Parochial School Runs into Trouble

Government gradually took more interest in education as the nineteenth century rolled on. The church school movement was at first suspicious of government grants, believing that education was the business of the church rather than the state. But by the time of Norris's death, the National Society was accepting Government funding, and when in 1870 the new London School Board made elementary education compulsory the churches were keen to co-operate, realising that they would now increasingly be in competition with school board schools such as the nearby three-decker Lauriston Road and Orchard schools, built from the 1890s onwards. More accommodation was needed, and in 1873 South Hackney parish, supported by a National Society grant and voluntary subscriptions, spent £464 on building onto the school in Percy Road an extension for 150 infants.[94] Again, St Thomas's Hospital helped by donating land for the new building. A further extension was built in 1884, bringing the accommodation to three large rooms and five smaller classrooms. By the end of the century, nearly five hundred children were being taught in these eight rooms.

Although compulsory, elementary education was not yet free: in South Hackney in 1888, schooling for an infant cost two pence a week while older children paid three pence each, though no family was asked to pay more than one shilling a week in total. These fees came nowhere near covering the cost of running the school; fees for younger pupils at the Lady Holles' School, a local private school for girls, were £4 a year, or about 2/- a week.[95] Eight years later, the parochial school was in financial trouble: not only had fees been abolished in 1891, but the education department had required the toilets to be upgraded. A £300 debt was growing by £40 a year, and an appeal was needed to pay it off.

As befitted a church school, the first forty-five minutes of each day for every pupil was devoted to religious instruction. The school's performance in this area was inspected by the diocese, not by the Government's inspectorate. The educational quality of this work may be gauged from the inspectors' 1895 comment that 'throughout the school, the repetition work has been very successfully prepared.'

Most of the money being spent on education was now coming from Government grants, but these were related to each school's success in official tests. Because church schools generally did less well in the tests than the better equipped and better staffed board schools, the financial problem was directly related to the problem of lower standards in church schools; it was a vicious circle. In South Hackney, the school inspectors' 1898 report showed that the situation in the boys' section of the church school certainly left much to be desired. 'This school is too little under the supervision of the Head Master, who is the only certificated teacher on the staff', it said, adding 'This should be remedied.' The inspectors also found that while 'some of the work is creditably done ... the first standard is not satisfactory'. This was hardly surprising, for several of the fifteen teaching staff were 'pupil-teachers', young people learning to be teachers by assisting in the classroom. Even allowing for the more abrasive style of the day, the inspectors had clearly identified an unacceptable state of affairs, but the remedy was really out of local hands; a national restructuring of education was needed, and eventually came in 1902. In these circumstances, it is perhaps surprising that Rector Dodd, did what he could to shame his school by publicising its shortcomings in the church magazine. But then, Dodd had more than a little sympathy for the board schools, of which he and his curates were prepared to serve as managers. He even remarked that their non-denominational 'religious teaching is in many ways good.'[96]

James Tossell had been head of the boys' school since 1880; on his death aged only 48 in 1902, the inspectors generously modified their view of his achievements: 'The school is in very good order and the work in every class well up to date,' they said, and hoped the new head would maintain the school's 'high reputation.' The following year however they noted that the new head master, Gilbert Prin, had 'thrown new life and vision into the school' and raised attendances by seven percent.[97] Prin too spent most of his career in the South Hackney parochial schools, including 19 years as head of the boys' department.

The Parochial Charities

When it was created in 1824, the parish of South Hackney had inherited both a share of the ancient parish of Hackney's charitable endowments and responsibility for the Monger-Martin almshouse. Some property continued to be managed by St John-at-Hackney on behalf of all three parishes. As had been the tradition for centuries, all the parochial charities continued to be administered by the Rector and Churchwardens; management was relatively informal. This informality sometimes led to laxity. Soon after Lockwood became Rector, he realised that the charities' affairs needed radical reform, and formed a committee to make recommendations. George Wales and William Norris were members of the committee. Expert they certainly were, but whether they were wholly independent is open to doubt; Wales already held strong views about the way the trustees of the parochial charities discharged their responsibilities, and Norris was a major local builder.

The committee proposed a series of far-reaching changes. For ease of administration the various bread, coal, meat, potatoes and other funds should be consolidated into a single fund. Responsibility for managing the charities should lie with a standing committee of seven, including the Rector and churchwardens. A number of legal irregularities needed to be put right with the cooperation of the authorities at St John-at-Hackney. Finally, it felt that the income-producing estate was not being effectively managed by St John-at-Hackney: not only were rents too low, but some land swaps with other landowners were needed to prepare the way for the letting of building leases when current pasturage leases expired. By way of promoting the needed reforms, these recommendations were published in a booklet in 1856,[98] but the proposals were not implemented for many years.

Meanwhile another struggle over the parochial charities was taking place.[99] Until the 1850s, the only local authorities had been the Anglican church and the magistrates. With the setting up of the Metropolitan Board of Works and its elected governing body, it became necessary to sort out which of the ancient responsibilities of the local rectors and churchwardens should be transferred to the new secular authorities. The new authority attempted to wrest control of South Hackney's parochial charities from the church. The Commissioners of Charities decided in favour of leaving the charities under church control in the time-honoured fashion. Whether this was entirely wise may be doubted, for in 1869 an exposé in the local *Hackney and Kingsland Gazette* – presumably the result of a leak by an interested party – alleged that the Hackney charities as a whole were spending significantly more on administration than they were distributing to the poor.

By 1894, order had been imposed on the charities. A committee of householders was assisting the Rector and churchwardens in their management, and only three percent of the charities' income was being spent on administration. The separate funds except those supporting the two almshouses were being treated as a single generalised charity fund. In that year, out of an income of £472, grants totalling £21 were made to the almshouses, and the parish provident societies and various local hospitals were each given about the same amount; £94 was used in the direct relief of poverty, half of it being given in the form of vouchers for such items as meat, bread, coal and

A POET IN THE PARISH: REV. WALTER JOHN FERRAR MA

W J Ferrar was curate at South Hackney under Vivian Lennard from 1893 to 1895.[100] He had studied at Hertford College, Oxford, and won the university's Newdigate poetry prize in 1891. His first collection of poetry, *Fritillaries*, was published in 1892. The poems reproduced here come from *Sacred Poems* of 1903 and seem to reflect experience gained in South Hackney; by then he was vicar of St Philip, Bethnal Green. He continued to publish poetry and theological and devotional works throughout his life.

A Hymn for Queen Victoria's Diamond Jubilee, 1897

This hymn is remarkable for dealing, albeit obliquely, with the fact that a queen celebrating her Diamond Jubilee cannot be far from death. It was published in a special collection of hymns for the Jubilee, set to a tune by South Hackney's organist, John E West. It was sung at St John of Jerusalem church at the end of evensong on the Sunday of the Jubilee, 20 June 1897.

Ah, sweet the sunset glow
   Among the western skies –
And sweet at eventide the flow
   Of glorious memories.

As God hath blest the day
   With gladdening warmth and light,
He bids his children calm to stay
   Awaiting restful night.

Now in a solemn strain
   Around the palace door
Thanksgiving for the glorious reign
   To gracious Heaven soar.

Thine, Father, all the praise!
   And from Thy Heaven serene
With peaceful light of sunset rays
   Still bless, still save the Queen.

The Prodigal Son

The parable of the prodigal son fascinated Ferrar throughout his life: he published 'The Gospel in the Gospel – a short study of the parable of the prodigal son' in 1945. This is the complete poem. Is there an echo here of Lennard's teaching about the need to develop responsible independence in children?

He will be *free*, so riots, till the stern
   Goads of strange sins force him to turn again;
He'll be his father's *slave* – oh, late to learn
   That fathers wish their sons not slaves, but men.

The Question

Victorian sentimentality certainly, but it reflects the very real precariousness of young life at the time.

'If I pray to God, mother,
   Will he hear me praying?
In his heaven far away
   Will he know what I am saying?'

So the tiny sufferer asked,
   Clasping hands demurely,
And she answered, answered low:
   'Darling, he will hear you surely.'

'If I ask Him e'er so softly
   Will He make me well?'
She can only weep and kiss him;
   'Ask not that! I cannot tell.'

Retrorsum

Ferrar reflects on how rewarding he finds his ministry in the 'lowly homes' of east London compared with his time as a student in the 'cloisters' of Oxford.

I turned me from the trodden road,
   I sought the cloisters of the wise,
Who, in calm thought's serene abode
   Track errant truth with fearless eyes.

Ah me! What forthright winding wild
   Led on my steps by waning light!
How nearer wisdom is the child
   Than he who scales her mountain height.

God called me from the darkening quest;
   He called me, and I turned again.
I turned me, tired and craving rest,
   To lowly homes and humble men.

I found Him seated as of old,
   'Mid labouring men and toil-worn wives;
I saw Him in His blessing fold
   The little hours of childish lives.

And often I have I seen Him stand
   In darkened rooms when women wept,
And smooth the pillows with His hand
   And tell them that their brother slept.

With lowly friends He loved to rove,
   'Neath cottage roofs His seat was set;
Not strangely, then, 'mid faith and love
   Of simple lives I find Him yet.

potatoes. As various parts of the parish were split off from South Hackney, the trustees made grants to the new vicars from the charitable funds, thus ensuring that the whole of the southern part of the ancient Hackney parish continued to benefit from the legacies. This approach had been officially backed by the Commissioners of Charities in 1867, soon after the first of the South Hackney's daughter parishes had been created.

The giving of assistance to the needy in accordance with the various charitable bequests was a highly public activity. In 1883, for example, advertisements were posted around the parish asking those who wished to receive help from the Marlowe, Powell and Digby funds to present themselves at the parochial school with details of their situation. The advert made clear that applicants could be resident in any part of the original parish of South Hackney. The personal details submitted were then printed, with names attached, and issued to the 150 or so rate-paying parishioners who attended a special church Vestry meeting to vote on which cases should receive what help. There could be no complaint that the business was not transacted openly, but perhaps the very openness of the process helps to explain why receiving charity came to be so resented by the people who had no option but to rely on it.

Management of the almshouses continued along the lines that the Williams case had illustrated in 1851. A late nineteenth century list of the Rules of Monger's Almshouse has survived. Among the rules we find: 'The inmates to be within their houses before Eleven o'clock at night, and to be careful to extinguish their fires and candles. The outer gate to be locked at eleven o'clock at night.' The rules deal in advance with cases like George Williams': inmates are to be sober, and any violation of any of the rules will result in dismissal. It seems that at least one resident, John Cockshutt, fell foul of this rule, and curiously his case was doubly similar to Williams' for he too had allowed his sister-in-law to stay in the almshouse; warned in October 1878 that he must cease his scandalous behaviour, by the following June he had left the almshouse and his place was being filled.[101]

The trustees were careful to fulfil to the letter the terms of the bequests they administered. So, in 1880, wanting to admit John Jackson to Monger House even though he had recently moved out of South Hackney to neighbouring Homerton, they took advice on the matter and were told that almsmen must be parishioners at the time of appointment. The offer to Jackson was withdrawn.[102] Similarly, when an almsman who had been living in Monger House with his wife died in 1895, his wife was given a month to vacate the property; it is not recorded whether or not a place was found for her at Norris House, though census returns show that widows of Monger's almsmen did sometimes move out into Norris House on the death of their husbands. Few residents lived in the almshouses for more than ten years, and those who did naturally tended to be women. Census returns also show that Norris House residents occasionally had someone living with them as their servant-cum-nurse.

The parish was equally scrupulous in ensuring that all possible applicants for places in the almshouses had the opportunity to apply; when a vacancy occurred notices inviting applications were posted round the parish. It takes an effort to imagine the relief an elderly person making a precarious living would feel on being appointed for the remainder of life to a safe home and a pension. Yet demand for places in Monger House seems to have fallen, for whereas in the mid-1870s there were usually about ten applicants for each vacancy, twenty years later, there was sometimes only one, and the number of 'notices of vacancy to be sent to all places of worship in the original parish of South Hackney and placed in the shop windows in each of the principal streets' was raised to five hundred.[103]

At the Turn of the Century

Despite all the multifarious activities in and around churches, the Anglican church continued to feel threatened. In the 1890s, frequent articles appeared in the South Hackney parish magazine about 'church defence' against the threat to church schools and against the threat of Anglican disestablishment in Wales. There was a nationwide petition against the latter and, in these days before women had the vote, Rector Lennard thought it helpful to remind readers that 'persons of either sex are entitled to sign'. Yet all this seemed to miss the point. Such threats – and even the challenge represented by the local 'hall of Progress so called ... opened by secularists' in the 1880s – were not the greatest danger to the church in South Hackney. That, as the clergy sometimes recognised, was indifference among the population at large.[104]

Just occasionally, amongst all the information we have about services and music and buildings and activities, we get a glimpse of what the people who took part in church life in the 1890s actually believed. Having in 1895 invited himself back to St John of Jerusalem to preach, Walsham How, by now Bishop of Wakefield, dwelt 'forcibly on the fact of our Lord's Risen Body having personal identity with that which was nailed to the cross.' Again, at the dedication festival in 1896, the dean of Bristol preached about religious

Dreamed-of spire. The tower and soaring spire shown in this view of Christ Church, Gore Road, were never built, proving once again – like the St John of Jerusalem crossing vault – that what is not done to start with is rarely done afterwards.
Parish magazine, 1902   Courtesy of Dr Melvyn Brooks

1851 to around 1900: A Flourishing Victorian Parish

doubt: he said that 'Doubt on the most essential truths of Christianity was very common. It was felt by many regular church-going people. If it made men think, it might result in good, and lead men to the strong rock of faith, but in itself it was paralysing.'[105] These preachers were acknowledging that, for all the busy-ness of church life, there was by the 1890s plenty to unsettle the minds of church-goers. On the whole, however, it was still intellectual: unchanging religious faith seemed to be under attack both externally from post-Darwin scientists and internally from biblical scholars, but it did not seem to suffer from any essential spiritual inability to speak to the human condition. So, as the Victorian era drew to its close, South Hackney church people could have found sufficient reasons to be confident that the church life they knew was secure. This confidence was neatly symbolised by Christ Church, whose parish magazine in the early years of the new century showed the church with the tall spire that was planned but, as it turned out, never built.

Chapter III

Around 1900 to the 1970s: Lean Years

Adverse Conditions

Several elements combined to make much of the twentieth century difficult for St John of Jerusalem church. One had been creeping up for several years and was entirely local; the others erupted on South Hackney as a result, directly or indirectly, of developments on the European mainland.

Already in 1895, the church magazine was commenting on the 'rapid social deterioration' that was taking place as the large, handsome houses in Well Street were turned into boot and shoe factories. It happened by accident: the trustees of St Thomas's Hospital, which owned much of the land south of Well Street, were less careful than their counterparts of the Cass Charity in preventing multiple occupation and changes of use in leased property. What had been a socially diverse parish became ever more homogeneous as the new century wore on. Middle class villas were divided for multiple occupation or pulled down to be replaced by Council flats for people who could not afford to buy or rent their homes on the open market. Like the people of the old St Andrew's mission district, they tended to be less interested in church activities than the people they displaced. This contributed to, though it did not wholly explain, a marked decline in church attendance. Between 1886 and 1903 – well before the Great War had had its shattering effect on traditional religious faith – attendance at St John of Jerusalem church, Christ Church and St Andrew's mission church had fallen by almost half.[106]

The purchasers of the few houses which were built in the parish during this period, particularly Meynell Gardens and Sharon Gardens in the 1930s, or which changed hands, also tended not to attend church. As Rector Cecil wrote in October 1935, 'The beginning of 1933 marked the highest point reached in attendances, financial strength, etc. [at St John of Jerusalem since Cecil arrived in 1930]. Since then however we have been passing through a testing time. Family after family have moved out from us to the new districts which are growing up all round London. Their houses have been taken by Jewish people, so that the Jewish population of the parish which was about 5% in 1930, is now estimated at about 50%. The wonder is that we have any congregation left at all.' Cecil's figures are unreliable, but the movement was broadly as he described it. It was, of course, not surprising that the Jewish people who moved to South Hackney from Tower Hamlets and further afield attended synagogue rather than church.

To these demographic changes were added the effects of war and its aftermath. When war erupted in August 1914, no-one in South Hackney would have suspected that the cloud that then descended on Europe was going to blight most of the rest of the century. The Great War was not only unimaginably costly in blood and treasure; it undermined many of the old assumptions about faith and about society. And it was followed by a depression which went beyond economics, and which ended only when another war brought destruction to South Hackney as if it had been on the front line. The awfulness of all this combined with the uncertainties of the Cold War to devalue what had been inherited from before disaster struck in 1914, a devaluation which drastically altered South Hackney, including its parish church.

Perhaps it is a measure of the mood in these years that relatively few church documents have survived. What has survived to witness to the tale of damage and destruction in South Hackney is the church building itself. Between 1848 and 1900, practically all the changes made to the building were improvements, enrichments or repairs. By the 1970s, almost all the original windows had gone, the stone spire had gone, the choir stalls had gone, the pulpit and lectern had gone, the benches in the aisle had gone, the organ was damaged beyond repair, and even the gravestones outside had mostly been destroyed. Tellingly, the only entirely fresh addition was the War Memorial outside the west door.

War and Post-War

The Edwardian years leading up to the Great War had a curious atmosphere; the Victorian settlement was crumbling and there was the foreshadowing of war, yet the outward forms of stability remained in place. One of the post-war rectors of South Hackney, the Irishman Francis Doherty, had published

THE RINGING OF THE BELLS

In the bell chamber twenty metres up in the tower hang eight bells, all cast by C and G Mears of Whitechapel and together weighing four tons. Over the century-and-a-half since they were installed, they have sometimes hung silent for years at a time, ready to peal forth when a new group of enthusiasts for what they call the Exercise feels the urge to take part in the uniquely English practice of change-ringing, dating from the seventeenth century. The order in which eight bells can be rung can be changed in what mathematicians call 'factorial eight' (written as 8!) times before any order has to be repeated. 8! equals $8 \times 7 \times 6 \times 5 \times 4 \times 3 \times 2 \times 1$, or 40320, so there is plenty of scope for ringing the changes. To ring one eighth of these one after another, making the changes in a patterned way, is to ring a 'peal', and there are many different evocatively named patterns, including South Hackney Surprise Major. Full 'peals' can take well over three hours and are rarely performed and carefully recorded, often on painted peal boards in the ringing chamber; 'quarter-peals' are commoner, and a 'touch' can be completed in a matter of minutes. Controlling heavy bells at the end of a rope so that they ring in the right order is not easy; the South Hackney ringing chamber offers an additional challenge in that some forty centimetres above the floor the drive shafts for the three clock faces on the tower cross the chamber. It seems that the clock was an afterthought that architect Hakewill had not foreseen.

One of the first recorded peals at St John of Jerusalem was rung as a funeral tribute to him whom the ringers called, with pardonable inaccuracy, 'the late lamented the Rev H H Norris, 42 years Rector of this Parish.' Further peals were rung during the 1850s, some by the local team, others by visitors who included the Ancient Society of College Youths. But in the 1880s, the bells fell silent, presumably because of concerns for the safety of the spire.

Having secured the spire, Rector Dodd, encouraged no doubt by Charles Winkley his bellringing churchwarden, saw to it that the bells were rehung and brought back into use in 1909; the number 2 bell was also recast. The touch of Grandsire Triples to mark the rededication was conducted by M A Wood, who had been one of

> the ringing team when the first peal was rung in 1848; the Exercise had clearly done him no harm! At least fourteen peals were rung before the Great War silenced bells across the land.
>
> In December 1919, a peal of Stedman Triples 'was rung on the second anniversary of the fall of Jerusalem. All the ringers served in His Majesty's Forces during the Great War in those campaigns which resulted in the overthrow of the Turk and the surrender of the Holy City.' Perhaps the ringers, from the Hertfordshire association of ringers, had been drawn to make their commemoration here by the mention of Jerusalem in the church's dedication as much as by the fine set of bells. Further peals were rung throughout the 1920s and '30s. Having survived through the church's lean years, the Exercise disappeared in South Hackney in the late 1960s; the team's last recorded ring was a half muffled tribute to Sir Winston Churchill on his death in 1965.
>
> In 1979, the South Hackney Society of Church Bell Ringers was revived. As well as ringing regularly before Sunday services, the society's members saw to it that peals were once again heard from the St John of Jerusalem bells. The tradition continued, and quarter-peals were rung on special occasions, including one of Plain Bob Doubles to mark the Queen's visit to the rebuilt Kingshold housing estate near the church in 1998 and one of Plain Bob Minor for the re-opening of Norris House in 2002.

a book of sermons in 1911 entitled *Sunshine in Religion* in which he emphasised his belief in 'a bright, joyful Christianity'. Such determined but somewhat insensitive optimism seems in retrospect to have something in common with the comment by the leader of the South Hackney Church Lads Brigade in connection with the South African War a few years earlier. He wrote that 'to our disgust, no orders have been received hitherto from the War Office for our mobilisation, and our new khaki uniforms have not arrived.' Even the rector had written, at the same time, that 'we do not forget that to die in obedience to the call of duty is the most honourable and glorious of deaths.' Such was the mood in which many South Hackney church people prepared for the coming of war in 1914.

The rector for the most of the Great War was the only one so far to become a bishop. Basil Staunton Batty had studied at Selwyn College, Cambridge, and was a Fellow of the Royal Astronomical Society. He stayed in South Hackney for less than four years; for much of that time he served as chairman of the Bishop of London's Council for Work in Munitions Centres, for which he was made an Officer of the Order of the British Empire. He left South Hackney for a West End parish in 1918. In 1926, he became bishop for North and Central Europe, giving episcopal support to the isolated Anglican churches that had grown up wherever diplomacy, trade or leisure drew sufficient English people. He was variously honoured: as well as being an OBE and a Lambeth Doctor of Divinity, he was admitted to the Orders of the Crown of Italy, of the Star of Roumania and of the Dannebrog.

Back at St John of Jerusalem, life went on less glamorously. Like every other community in Europe, South Hackney was trying to deal with the aftermath of war. A war memorial in the form of a white stone cross was erected outside the west door of the church; instead of the names of the dead of the parish it bore a bronze plaque with an inscription which seems not to have freed itself from pre-war attitudes: 'In memory of the Parishioners who for the Faith and Honour of Christendom died gloriously for ENGLAND 1914–1919'. One wonders what the soldiers' bereaved families made of such a sentiment. The Cornells, for example, who put up a tablet in the church recording the deaths of two sons killed in action in France in the summer of 1916 as well as those of two other sons who died the following year. Or Charles and Maud Winkley, whose son went to war when he was only 16 and was killed late in 1917 before he reached 20; the Military Cross he had won was included on his memorial tablet. These families were churchgoers; the Cornell memorial notes that the young men were baptised and confirmed at St John of Jerusalem, and Captain Winkley's father was both a churchwarden and a bellringer, as well as a past Mayor of Hackney. Perhaps they reflected on the bitter irony that the church's 'new crusade against all impurity', the Church Lads' Brigade, had in effect trained a generation of young men for the obscenity of the trenches. They and the millions of families like them could not be expected to accept with equanimity the man-made slaughter of war; many found it harder than they had before August 1914 to find the God in whom they had been taught to believe.

The war also affected social attitudes, which impacted upon the Church of England as much as the rest of society. The increased appetite for democratic accountability ended the centuries old power of the Rector and his Churchwardens by instituting the Parochial Church Councils; South Hackney had been ahead of its time in electing an informal council in the 1890s.[107] As

The War Memorial, erected after the Great War of 1914 to 1918 but never updated to remember the dead of later wars.
Photograph by Geoff Taylor

women's social role outside of the home was recognised generally, the new PCCs had women as full members, though permission for deaconesses to be styled 'Reverend' and to be allowed to preach had to wait until after the Second World War. The financial legacy of the Great War meant that clergy along with other middle class people were required to pay more tax than before. On top of that, the old pew renting system that had at first been so significant a part of clergy income was finally ended in South Hackney by Henry Cecil in 1932, soon after his appointment as rector; it would certainly have offended his egalitarian principles.[108]

As finances were stretched, it was desirable that the Rector of South Hackney be housed less opulently than in the large 1870s Rectory, with its provision and need for several servants. In 1930, the old building was sold to

The view from the pew in the 1930s. Several prominent features seen here were not to survive the imminent war, notably the organ, the windows and the stencilling.
Courtesy of Hackney Archives Department

Toc H for £3,100. The money was donated by Punch magazine, which lent its name to the house in its new guise as a hostel for young men. Founded by army chaplain Tubby Clayton in Flanders in 1916, Toc H had a natural affinity with the church, and the relationship between St John of Jerusalem and the hostel was a close one for many years. Rector Cecil lived there while a more modest new rectory was built on what remained to the church of the large garden of the old rectory.[109]

The state of the church building imposed another strain on the inadequate resources of a parish eighty per-cent of whose population was regarded as poor. In 1932, Cecil wrote to the Incorporated Church Building Society seeking financial help, telling them that 'I was appointed Rector of South Hackney eighteen months ago, and found the Church building in a very neglected and in some places dangerous condition.' He had already collected the funds necessary to carry out the most urgent repairs, to the roof and the interior; he now needed help to deal with the flaking ragstone exterior. The work cost £1200, of which the ICBS gave £40; the collection at a special service for Freemasons raised a further £87 towards the stonework repairs.

In the recently revived church magazine in November 1931, Rector Cecil asserted – with, one suspects, more hope than conviction – that 'Our Church at South Hackney is not "dead and done for" as so many seem to have thought. It is very much alive and is beginning again to take its place more fully in the life of this great district.' At the very least, it is clear that the twenties had stood in sharp contrast to the confident Victorian years, and as it turned out the rector saw his hopes dashed. Some things stayed the same: there were still three services each Sunday, with sung communion following matins twice a month. The Sunday School and Women's Bible Class continued, as did the slightly re-named Young Men's Club. There were enough choir members to make a reasonable attempt to sing West's anthems from time to time. And it was possible to leave the church open each day for prayer and meditation without much risk of vandalism.

But as the number of ordinations fell by two-thirds after the war, so in South Hackney the clergy count was down from five to two; more reliance was necessarily placed on the three 'lady workers' living together in Meynell Crescent. Services ceased to be held at St Andrew's mission church, and the building was turned into a parish hall, with the hope that its congregation would go instead to St John of Jerusalem church. There were other changes in the weekly round: a Mother's Union branch was belatedly opened, in parallel with a Women's Fellowship, and Boy Scouts and Cubs temporarily replaced the Church Lads' Brigade, making it natural for provision to be made for Girl Guides and Brownies.

All Saints House proved unsustainable. The old building was sold and demolished in 1934, when the memorial to Mother Alice was moved from its chapel to the north transept of St John of Jerusalem church. On its site, the twenty-one new houses of Meynell Gardens were built, their front gardens walled with the rubble of the old house.

Throughout these inter-war years, there seems to have been a sense of bravely trying to keep the Anglican show on the road in South Hackney as local changes combined with the mood of the times and grim developments on a national and international level to weaken the church.

War on the Doorstep

Unlike the docks and *materiel* factories, South Hackney was not a strategic target for German bombing in the Second World War, but the morale of its people was the target of terror bombing during the blitz in 1940.[110] Landmines

RESPONSES TO WAR: REHABILITATION AND RECONSTRUCTION

The dislocation and disorientation produced by the Great War provoked vastly differing responses across Europe and beyond. Two of the clergy who served South Hackney during its lean years exemplified aspects of this variety within the church.

Lambert Foxell had served as a military chaplain during the war, and became as a result a lifelong Honorary Chaplain to the Forces, entitled to display richly embroidered royal crowns on his preaching scarf. No doubt his wartime experiences informed his deep concern for stability, and perhaps that in turn helps explain why he remained Vicar of Christ Church, Gore Road for over thirty years. In his extra-parochial activities, it manifested itself in his commitment to the Royal Martyr Church Union, of which he was chaplain. The RMCU had been founded in 1906 to promote the official observance by the Church of England of the anniversary of the execution of King Charles I on 30 January 1649.

Vicar Foxell preached at the Union's annual service at St Martin in the Fields on 30 January 1950, recounting the beheading of Charles as a 'helpless victim of a Junta of plutocratic bosses. ... In the name of Justice we call that murder; in the name of Christ we call it martyrdom; for had he loved the Church less – had he abjured his faith and signed the Solemn League and Covenant he would not have died thus. His enemies called that Obstinacy – others call it loyalty to his Faith and to his Church. But we do not venerate his memory simply because he was loyal to his Church; we do so for a higher reason even than that. We revere him as a great and noble Christian Gentleman who had God ever before his eyes and who quietly yielded up his soul to his Maker and his Redeemer in the face of a travesty of justice and of hypocritical enemies. Verily "he endured grief, suffering wrongfully" [I Peter 2 v 29] and whether or not the powers that be allow his name to be printed once again in the Calendar from which it has been quite illegally and rather disgracefully omitted, we of the Royal Martyr Church Union, in common with all who have acquainted themselves with Truth, know that his name is blessed for evermore in the Calendar above, writ in letters of gold among the noble Army of Martyrs.'[111]

This was not a matter of merely antiquarian interest or of seeing justice belatedly done; to support the RMCU was to defend values its members believed were threatened: the Faith of the Church, Loyalty to the Crown and Liberty for the People. It was also to oppose the Liberal version of English history as steady progress under the leadership of socially sensitive if not necessarily socialist intellectuals. By contrast, **Henry Cecil** wished to see the church in the vanguard of the social forces working to create a better environment for human flourishing than the world that war seemed to have destroyed. He brought to his ministry as Rector of South Hackney the convictions he had formed in Sheffield between 1913 and 1930.

Around 1920, with colleagues who included Baptist, Congregational and Methodist ministers, he co-edited *Brightest England and the Way In* to promote an approach to post-war Reconstruction in poor, working-class parishes such as his own at St Philip's, Sheffield. It relied on volunteers, including young people living at the local YMCA 'settlement' or hostel, who would regularly visit impoverished families. No questions were asked concerning the volunteers' 'private views about society and the universe'; indeed, Cecil and his friends were happy to say that 'We do not find it necessary, dear reader, to worry about theology'. The aim of these visits was to 'tell the people of St Philip's that the War has brought to an end nineteenth century greed and cruelty, filth and shame, and that men and women are at once going to create a social order based upon universal comfort and culture and fellowship… The final fundamental aim of every effort we make is that of forcing individuals to recognise that "the Kingdom of God is within them". The psychic phenomenon of which we are thinking goes by a score of names. "Awakening" is perhaps as good as any. We regard the mass of people of St Philip's (more in proportion of the well-to-do than of the many poor) as *asleep* – ignorant of what life really is, indifferent to serious things, unable to appreciate the purest joys, unaware of their right to fine ways of living.'[112] In South Hackney, Rector Cecil helped establish a settlement run by Toc H,

> an organisation whose ethos and approach were strikingly similar to those advocated by him in Sheffield. One is left wondering what the poor of Sheffield or later of South Hackney made of this assault, well intentioned as it undoubtedly was.
>
> Cecil's willingness to work with non-churchmen went beyond the non-conformists, and he claimed the support of political left wingers such as G D H Cole, H M Hyndman and Bernard Shaw. He strongly backed the Labour Movement because 'the motive (certainly of the best element in the movement) is not merely a selfish craving for material gain; rather it is a desire for the advantages, educational, spiritual, etc., which these material things may bring, a desire for that fullness of life which Christ meant all men to have.'[113]
>
> No doubt these contemporary neighbouring Anglican incumbents would have had much to discuss. Cecil may have been more ambitious than Foxell, but who is to say which of the two was the more successful? The Church of England's *Alternative Service Book* of 1980 included in its list of Lesser Festivals and Commemorations the date of the execution of 'Charles I, King, Martyr, 1649.'

were massively destructive bombs; the one that landed on the old St Andrew's mission district ripped out its heart with blast and fire. When the war was over there was no option but to tear down what remained and build anew. The result of this rebuilding was the Frampton Park Estate of local authority housing. The old mission church itself – which had been used by the congregation of the Mare Street Baptist church following its destruction by bombing a few months earlier – was on the edge of the affected area and it was decided to sell the site to the Council.

Another 1940 bomb landed in Church Crescent, a little way south of St John of Jerusalem church. It severely damaged houses on both sides of the road, necessitating the building of the small Banbury Estate by the Council in the 1960s. Both the old and new rectories and Monger's Almshouse suffered varying amounts of blast damage. The blast also reached the church, making the already-weak spire still more dangerous, damaging the south-facing roofs and buttresses, and blowing out the windows. A few of the original windows on the west and north sides that were small enough to withstand the blast remain, sparkling like unexpected jewels and giving some idea of what was lost. The damage was not over in one night; the damp that was now able to penetrate the building continued unseen to corrode the organ. The body of the church had to be abandoned except for occasional services; ordinary services were held in a windowless chapel formed within the north transept,[114] attended by rarely more than thirty worshippers. With the church damaged and the hall and clubhouse permanently out of action, many church activities could continue only by courtesy of Mr W P Forbes, who made his house at 13 Groombridge Road available to the church until 1950.

Bombs also hit the area south of Well Street, and among the buildings damaged beyond permanent repair was the young men's clubhouse in what had by now been renamed Kingshold Road; Norris Almshouse was less seriously damaged. Christ Church was slightly damaged by the bombs that destroyed the houses that stood between Victoria Park Road and the western end of the Park. Towards the end of the war, the church school was seriously damaged by V2 flying bomb, and St Augustine's church was bomb-damaged. Bad as they were, things could have been much worse: five V1 flying bombs landed just inside Victoria Park, thus failing to wreak the Vengeance that had been their only purpose.

Struggling On

The end of hostilities revealed that the physical damage was only the most visible legacy of war. On the positive side, there was a national determination to try, this time, to provide proper health care, housing, education and social security for everyone. But there was a negative side too, like the explosion in divorce; in May 1946, the parish magazine was reporting the church's worried response to the 45,000 marriages that were under threat from returning servicemen's divorce petitions.

South Hackney parish, like everyone else, tried to pick up the threads of pre-war life. Much had changed. There was now just the rector, Richard Parsons, working without any full time support. The Sunday school ceased to be held on Sunday afternoons because teachers could not be found; the children now received instruction after matins in the morning. The Scouts faded away, to be replaced in the late 1950s at the instance of Rector Isherwood, a former Navy chaplain, by a temporarily-revived Church Lads

Brigade. Various social activities, such as the Dramatic Society and parish orchestra, were started or revived. But they caused a certain amount of unease, since it was noticed that participants were not always regular church attenders. In the church magazine in February 1951, Rector Parsons attempted to deal with the question of whether parties, sports clubs, whist drives and so on could 'help the real work of the church.' Lurking behind this was a huge question to which the answer had seemed clear enough in the 1890s, when we found Rector Dodd saying that attendance at the Mother's Meeting ought to lead naturally to attendance at church. It seems that for Parsons things were not so straightforward, for he gives a kind of holding reply: we put fun and games in their proper place; faith and devotion come first.

The parish magazine itself changed: in the late 1940s, Parsons used it to try to bring a serious spiritual message to non-church-going readers, and as a well-qualified academic theologian he attempted to interest his readers in such topics as Existentialism, but he was also happy to print many jokes, which his nineteenth century predecessors would certainly have frowned upon. By the mid-'50s, it had shrunk to a single, duplicated sheet. Curiously but symptomatically, the picture on the cover of the magazine when it was revived again in the late 1950s showed the church with the stone spire, which had been removed in 1954.

Inevitably the choir had dwindled during the war. In 1950 there was a proposal for a choir of twenty boys to be paid to sing services once they had completed eighteen months training, but it seems unlikely that this came to fruition. Nevertheless under the firm and enthusiastic leadership of Joyce Levi and with Mr Bennett at the organ, much of the old ambition remained and choir membership reached thirty. Miss Levi's name proclaimed her Jewish origins; her father had come to Hackney from the collapsing Ottoman Empire after the Great War. She went to train as a teacher before returning and eventually becoming deputy head of Hackney Free and Parochial School. As well as performing anthems and such devotional music as *The Cross of Christ*, the choir took part in choral competitions. Despite Miss Levi's contribution from 1942 to 1964, there was a palpable reluctance to recognise women as full members of the choir, even after the changes brought about by the war; it was illustrated by a comment in the magazine in 1950: there was 'no special need for ladies of the choir to wear robes'.

Parsons hoped that it would be possible to rearrange the seating in the church so that there would be only four or five hundred places – 'quite enough if you want to get the real family spirit among those who worship', he wrote. And, he could have added, more than enough for the number of people who usually attend the church. Even nominal church membership was becoming less popular: baptisms fell from 186 in 1947 to only 124 two years later. In the July 1948 edition of the magazine, which covered the centenary celebrations of the church, he printed the headline 'Shall we scrap our church?' over an article lamenting how many people neither attended the church nor contributed to its upkeep but still wanted it to be there; perhaps some he had in mind were among those who turned up only to get married – there were still sometimes up to a dozen weddings on Saturdays. The centenary celebrations themselves drew a reasonable crowd, and were attended by the patron Lord Amherst and Colonel H Du C Norris, the first Rector's great-grandson, as well as the Mayor of the Metropolitan Borough of Hackney. Another major occasion was the 1956 service for nurses in memory of 'the illustrious Florence Nightingale', for which the church was packed.[115]

Despite this, the place of the church in local affections was less secure than it had been. In the early 1950s the rector had to ban children from the churchyard because of the deliberate damage they were inflicting on the church building, and two tons of lead were ripped from the church roof. Although vandals had overturned crosses in the churchyard in the 1890s, it is hard to imagine such events occurring during the years before the Second World War.

Some Damage is Repaired

The scale of material damage caused by the Second World War was such that extensive repairs to ordinary parish churches had to wait until the late 1940s and 1950s. In the meantime church-goers were naturally anxious to return to the church for regular services. So in 1946 'a good second-hand all-electric organ' was purchased as a temporary measure so that services could once again be held in the church. The damaged remains of the old organ were salvaged and in 1949 the organ builder Alfred E Davies combined them with parts of a second-hand Aeolian organ to produce a 'new', three manual organ with sixty stops. Fortunately the second-hand organ had been bought cheaply, for a great deal of costly work and ingenuity was needed for the rebuilding job.[116] Soon after it was installed in the tower, it was realised that there were pockets of still air, which allowed corrosion to take place; by the 1980s, the reconstituted organ was beyond economic restoration.

Some pre-war glass was fitted into the nave windows, where most of it remains. Some people regarded these plain windows with their green, wine and amber borders as an improvement; they made the church lighter. When it was possible to replace the transept and chancel windows, the hint seems to have been taken, for the coloured areas in the new windows were surrounded by generous amounts of clear glass. The new windows designed by Arthur Erridge were a triumph, and certainly far more interesting and thought-provoking than the geometrical patterns that had filled some of the windows before the war. The chancel windows took up the nursing theme suggested by the church's dedication to St John the Baptist thought of as patron saint of the Knights Hospitallers' hospital in Jerusalem. This turned out to be particularly fitting, since when the parish was enlarged a little later it took in the Roman Catholic St Joseph's Hospice, a pioneering centre for the care of the dying; as ecumenical relations warmed, the parish clergy became the Anglican chaplains to the Hospice.

The stone spire was unsafe and had to be removed in 1954. The cheap and easy option was to replace it with a flat roof adorned merely with a thin metal fleche.[117] This was, happily, rejected in favour of N F Cachemaille-Day's bolder contemporary design, a narrow spire the same height as its predecessor, whose copper sheathing would oxidise to an eye-catching bright green. The original finial representing the Lamb of God was replaced at the top of the new spire. While the roof of the tower was open, the opportunity was taken to lift out the bells so that the ringing frame could be repaired, with financial help from Colonel Norris; the normal route for removing the bells through trapdoors in every floor of the tower had carelessly been blocked when the organ had been built in the inadequately ventilated tower space. The nave roof on the south side that had suffered most from the bomb was also re-slated, using slates of a markedly greener tinge than the original ones. Unfortunately, the use of concrete as a filling where stone or mortar had crumbled allowed further and more serious damage to go on behind an apparently sound exterior.

An internal re-ordering was carried out at around the same time. The benches which had made sense of the wide aisle and which had had to be removed, for a small extra charge, every time a marrying couple wanted to enjoy the grandeur of the processional route, were finally got rid of. The wall of the chancel arcade was painted a rather chilly shade of light blue, decorated as before with the instruments of the Passion. And, for the first time, the church was equipped with a toilet, partitioned out of the original vestry, which became a primitive kitchen. One matter was overlooked however: no addition was made to the war memorial to commemorate the dead of Hitler's

Around 1900 to the 1970s: Lean Years

ARTHUR 'VIRGE' ERRIDGE MGPS, STAINED GLASS ARTIST

This feature is based on material collected by Francis Erridge

The artist responsible for the chancel and transept windows was Arthur Frederick Erridge. Unlike Hakewill and West, Erridge did not carry on a family artistic tradition. Born over a mews in 1899, he was the son of a Kensington coachman who died young, leaving his widow struggling to bring up six boys on her own. Erridge left school at 14 and would no doubt have had a quite different career had not the local vicar spotted his talent for drawing and found him a place at Powells stained glass studio, from where he went to train at the Central School of Arts and Crafts. Towards the end of the Great War, he served briefly in the navy before returning to Powells, where he remained, honing his skills, until the outbreak of the next world war put a temporary stop to stained glass work. Powells studio had a South Hackney connection: it took its name from James Powell, a South Hackney resident who took over the Whitefriars glassworks and who was related to Henry Handley Norris's wife, Catherine Powell.

During the new war, Erridge worked on engineering drawings for the Air Ministry and served as an Air Raid Protection warden. In his spare time he helped run the bomb victims' clearing centre at John Keble church in Mill Hill where his pre-war role of verger had already given him his nickname 'Virge'. Towards the end of the war, he moved his family to Suffolk where he did manual work. When after the end of the war Wippells of Exeter offered him freelance work as a stained glass designer once again, he had to overcome his serious doubts as to whether his wartime experiences had destroyed his artistic abilities.

They hadn't. Indeed, this was to be the beginning of a flourishing period in Erridge's life. Bombing had left many churches denuded of stained glass and other furnishings; there was great demand for his skills. These were not confined to stained glass design; an enormous wrought iron chandelier for Holy Trinity Church in Dalston was one of his works.

But it was stained glass where his skills shone most brightly. Between 1946 and his death in 1961, Erridge carried out commissions for windows throughout England, including several in Exeter Cathedral which earned approval even from Nikolaus Pevsner. As it happens, Hackney had more than its fair share of Erridge's work. His designs were installed in churches in Dalston, Stoke Newington and Upper Clapton as well as at South Hackney. But his largest commission was one of the thirty he received from across the Atlantic, that for thirty-eight windows for the chapel of the University of the South in Sewanee, Tennessee; some of them can be seen on its website.

Arthur Erridge
Courtesy of Francis Erridge

The South Hackney windows exemplify one of Erridge's guiding principles: the point of windows, even stained glass windows, was to let light into a building. He maintained that 'You can let in the light and have colour too', though some of his clients elsewhere seem to have insisted on dense colours with little clear glass. He was well aware of other artistic limitations imposed by his chosen medium; because of the painstaking process by which craftsmen slowly turned a design into a finished window, his was 'a disciplined art – you can't express yourself with absolute freedom.' But his advice to any would-be artist was clear: 'You must draw and draw and draw.'

At Wippells, Erridge was remembered as a kindly and Christian man. His family occasionally found his generosity and his undemanding approach to business affairs something of an irritant. But it was not only his artistry that earned him a fine memorial window in Marks Tey church near Colchester, illustrating Luke as the patron saint of artists painting a portrait of the Madonna and Child.

war. The church in South Hackney seems to have been unusually cavalier in dealing with the memory of those who had died in the world wars.

The loss of the parish hall in the old mission church in Well Street was not made good. There were plans to 'provide a properly equipped social centre staffed by church members to give young, middleaged and old folk of our parish facilities equal to any of similar scope where they may enjoy the best devotional, educational and recreational activities.' The proposed social centre was to have a large and a small hall, the former with a sprung dance floor, a youth section with gym, library and music room, class rooms for the Sunday school, a kitchen and even a hard tennis court. Such ambitions were well beyond the resources of the church, and seem in any case to have been framed with an idealised version of the pre-war world in mind.

The restored organ and new windows were dedicated at a special service in 1958, a few years into what was being optimistically called the new Elizabethan era, the reign of Elizabeth II. It turned out not to be the encouraging new start that was hoped for, either for South Hackney or for the country as a whole. The damage of the previous thirty years went deeper than could be fixed by material repairs or the coronation of a young monarch; indeed, more damage was to come.

Deliberate Destruction

The 1960s are perhaps too recent to be judged fairly yet. Nevertheless, it is undeniable that there was a great desire to clear away whatever seemed to constrain the future, whether it was buildings or social norms. It is facile to overlook the desperate and understandable desire to break free of a past that had been so unhappy for so long. But it was, as always, easier to pull things down than to create replacements that would be definite and lasting improvements.

In South Hackney, the mood led to several examples of what a later generation would regard as vandalism. Many of the undamaged mid-Victorian villas of King Edward's Road were torn down by the local authority, to be replaced by the Kingshold Estate of tower blocks and flat-roofed, concrete four-storey blocks connected by aerial walkways. Before they were themselves demolished in the 1990s, the estate had featured in a television series about the awfulness of life on a '60s Council estate, helping to give Hackney an unenviable national reputation.

No such publicity was given to what happened to the neighbouring church, mostly during the incumbency of James Isherwood, an Australian whose brother was chaplain at Hackney Hospital. The choir stalls that had been such an expensive and key feature of the church were removed from the chancel; a few years later the original altar fell into disuse in favour of an altar on the nave floor at the crossing which allowed Rector Hickley to celebrate the Eucharist facing the congregation. Though they reflect contemporary secular developments such as theatre-in-the-round, these changes had a theological rationale. In imitating the medieval church plan, Norris and Hakewill had unavoidably and unquestioningly encapsulated a medieval view of God and religion. As God was 'out there', in heaven, beyond us, transcendent, so his altar stood far away in a glorious setting, separated from the congregation by a robed choir and the clergy who seemed to be standing in for the heavenly host. It was about this 'out there' God that the miseries of the twentieth century, not to mention the earlier intellectual challenges, had caused many people to have doubts. In 1963, Bishop John Robinson published *Honest to God*, a book that appalled and reassured different groups of church-goers in almost equal measure. Part of Robinson's point was that in looking 'out there', people were failing to seek God within and among themselves. Obviously in seeking and worshipping this immanent God, a chancel such as Norris and Hakewill had provided represented more of a hindrance than a help. So it was abandoned and largely cleared of its furnishings.

It is less easy to make theological sense of Rector Isherwood's sudden and unauthorised destruction and removal of most of the gravestones in the graveyard, which had been closed for new graves since 1868 and in the care of Hackney Council since 1932. It was not uncommon in the 1960s to move headstones to the edges of graveyards and to level the humps and bumps that marked people's last resting places. It made the place neater and easier to keep tidy, though it also weakened the reminder of mortality that graveyards had long expressed in the centre of their communities. In the case of South Hackney, many of the broken stones found their way into nearby gardens as crazy paving. The stones that remain are presumably those that were too heavy to move, or perhaps not flat enough to provide paving; happily they include the grave of the first Rector and his wife, whose remains lie to the east of the apse.

Riddled with woodworm, the original wooden pulpit and lectern had to be disposed of. A rather unsuitable marble pulpit was obtained from Waltham Abbey and installed in 1964, but neither practical necessity nor implied meaning supported its use for very long. It seemed preposterous to address a dwindling congregation of little more than twenty from a pulpit two metres up in the air, and the replacement pulpit was soon returned to Waltham Abbey, where it was displayed in a public garden.

Suggestive of the mood of the day was a remarkable incident.[118] Following minor bomb damage, Christ Church had been demolished in 1948 and its parish was formally recombined with St John of Jerusalem parish in 1954, at the end of the thirty-one year incumbency of Lambert Foxell. The demolished church's fittings were eventually disposed of by the Rector of South Hackney, including a painting, which the Rector sold for the not inconsiderable sum of £1,000 to another Mr Foxell. This Mr Foxell then resold what he may perhaps already have suspected was something of a treasure for the enormous sum of £13,500. It is not clear from the records how this came to light, but when it did proceedings were issued against Mr Foxell in the name of the Attorney General and the Churchwardens for the return of the proceeds. In order to avoid unwelcome publicity, the defendant settled out of court in 1958. He handed over £9,500, half of which went to the diocese to offset what it had contributed to the post-war restoration; the rest became a useful investment for South Hackney parish.

The School

In 1902, peace broke out between the churches and the Government over the funding of church schools. It was agreed that the local authority would still not assist with the provision or updating of the church's school buildings, but would pay for wear and tear on the church's property when used for public elementary education, and also make a contribution to utilities costs. The sensitivity of the situation is illustrated by the nit-picking precision with which costs were apportioned between the local authority and the church. In South Hackney's case, the London County Council paid eighteen-nineteenths of the fuel bill;[119] presumably the other nineteenth was deemed to pay for heating lessons of religious instruction. Even more curiously, when the LCC provided a piano for the school it also issued a sliding scale of charges for occasions when the instrument was used for purposes not directly connected with public elementary education, such as the church Sunday school and classes for adults.[120]

As before, each year's grant was dependent on the school's success in the annual inspection by the LCC. In the early years of the century, South Hackney parochial school was said by the inspector to be generally in 'very good order', despite frequent observations that the school was severely

SOUTH HACKNEY'S WONDERFUL WINDOWS

St John of Jerusalem church lost many of its Victorian glories during the twentieth century. But the windows that replaced those blown out in the blitz are a worthy compensation and repay careful examination.

Installed in 1955, the widows of the transepts and chancel were paid for by the Government's War Damage Commission. They were made in Exeter by J Wippell and Company to designs by Arthur Erridge.

The seven lancets in the chancel refer to the medical and nursing work that the crusader Order of Knights of the Hospital of St John in Jerusalem carried out. The two windows on the north side show the Lady Agnes and Gerard. Agnes was a staunch supporter of the Order's Hospital, and the self sacrifice required is symbolised in the roundel above her by the pelican, which was believed in ancient times to feed its young with blood pecked from its own breast. Gerard was the founder and first Grand Master of the Order, and beneath him is a vignette showing aid being given to a crusader in the desert. Facing them are portraits of two more recent health-care heroes, Florence Nightingale and Albert Schweitzer. Florence holds a sheet of paper on which we may imagine she has written one of her trenchant letters to public officials demanding improvements in health care. In her roundel is the famous lamp that lighted her night-time rounds in the hospital she founded to serve soldiers suffering from the effects of the Crimean War. Schweitzer raised money for his mission hospital at Lambarene in Gabon, pictured in his vignette, by giving recitals on the organ, symbolised in his roundel. The book he holds represents his major books on Bach and the life of Jesus. It is noteworthy that Schweitzer was still alive when he was commemorated in this window.

The central panels of the three lancets of the apse illustrate a scene in the life of Jesus where he is healing the sick. The vignettes show Jesus talking with the Samaritan woman by the well, the crucifixion, and Moses healing people by showing them the serpent lifted up. The roundels are the crosses of England, the Order of Knights Hospitallers and Jerusalem.

The transept windows follow the customary scheme, with Old Testament figures in the north and Christian era figures in the south. The top of the Old Testament window illustrates Creation. In the large circular panel, the hand of God creates Adam and Eve in a burst of activity that includes the creation of the Earth and the stars. Beneath are the newly-created Sun and Moon. In the awkwardly shaped lights at the sides are seen, on the right, the serpent that beguiled Eve entwined in the branches of the tree of knowledge of good and evil, and on the left the angel with the flaming sword with which he expelled the unhappy couple from Eden after they had eaten of the tree's forbidden fruit.

The four main panels show Moses, Amos, Ezekiel and Jeremiah. Moses is shown with the tablets of the Ten Commandments and two shafts of light which represent how his face is said to have glowed; beneath he has his vision of the burning bush, while above him is, once again, the serpent he lifted up to heal the people. Amos the shepherd-prophet is shown holding a lamb; below the main panel, he is called by God as he follows his flock. The locust above him is, oddly, a symbol of hope, for in Amos's vision God threatens but does not bring about a famine caused by a plague of locusts. Ezekiel is wearing his priestly robes and swinging a smoking incense burner; in the vignette, he is seen before the candelabra in the Temple before going into the Exile, which is itself symbolised by the shackles above the main panel. Jeremiah is shown above a picture of him in the pit in which he was imprisoned on suspicion of being a fifth columnist during Nebuchadnezzar's siege of Jerusalem.

The south transept window shows, in the three circular panels between the first and last letters of the Greek alphabet, Jesus as Son of God, son of Mary, and resurrected Lord. The main panels mark a break with tradition by illustrating not New Testament scenes but eminent preachers of Christianity, starting with St Augustine of Hippo, one of the formative theologians of western

Christianity. He was particularly honoured by the Knights Hospitaller, and their parish church in Hackney was originally dedicated in his name. Next to him is Thomas Cranmer, the Archbishop of Canterbury who largely wrote the Anglican Book of Common Prayer and was eventually burnt as a heretic by the Catholic Queen Mary I; in the vignette below the main panel he is shown with colleagues working on the prayer book. Then comes the eighteenth century founder of Methodism, John Wesley, shown above a scene in which he is riding round industrial England on his endless preaching tours. Finally comes Archbishop William Temple, a major religious teacher in early twentieth century England. Above each figure is his coat of arms – Augustine would certainly have been surprised to find himself thus honoured!

Erridge's windows are fine examples of the art of stained glass. They also attempt to underline several teachings. They make it clear that the time of religious inspiration did not end centuries ago but continues to the present time, the time of Schweitzer and Temple. The unhistorical representation of Jesus as a beardless European is a now-outdated attempt to show him as 'one of us'. The chancel windows are clearly intended to give full value to women as active followers of Jesus.

The tradition of high quality stained glass has been continued with the installation of two windows in the nave. Designed by Susan Ashworth, they commemorate the lives of two long-serving members of the congregation. Dorothy and Arthur Baker belonged to the church from 1934 until their deaths in 1987 and 1994; between them they for many years held office as churchwarden, organist, choir member, and chair and clerk of the parochial charities. The windows represent much of their record of service: the church spire, the church school and the almshouses are easy to spot, as are the organ pipes weaving through the South Downs, an area they loved. Tiny portraits of Dorothy and Arthur are incorporated in the borders of the northern window.

understaffed and worked in buildings that were defective. Staffing at least had improved by the full inspection in 1930, but the seven-strong inspection team was unimpressed by the school's science teaching. They praised the part played by the school in the Hackney Music Festival, which also impacted on the school indirectly though the room hiring fees paid by the local choral society in the 1920s and '30s.[121]

In 1926, a major Government report on education, the Hadow report, recommended that all children should transfer to senior school at the age of 11. Many elementary schools, including South Hackney Parochial, took pupils right through to school leaving at age 14. The LCC put forward a scheme to bring its schools in South Hackney into line with the Hadow recommendations by 1932 and invited the church school to follow suit, giving up its senior pupils. On behalf of the managers, Rector Cecil brusquely turned down the carefully argued LCC proposal.[122] Part of the problem was that the LCC could give no guarantee that the senior places lost would be made up by junior age children, even though Lauriston Road school was overcrowded; parents' wishes as to which school their children attended had to be respected. The incident shows once again the delicacy of the church-state truce over education, and perhaps also an awareness on the part of the church that, given the choice, many parents would prefer their children to go to the newer and better-equipped local authority schools. The 1930 inspection had noted that, 'the children are for the most part rather poor and the provision of clothes and boots takes up a good deal of the head master's time'.[123] In the crude jargon of later decades, the parochial school was in danger of becoming an undesirable 'sink' school.

Part of the problem was that by the mid-1930s, the parochial school's main building was nearly eighty years old and had survived only by the addition of successive extensions. Apart from the problems caused by its age, its design was decades behind the teaching methods then being used. Rector Cecil was a prominent supporter of the Christian movement Conference on Politics, Economics and Citizenship, better known as COPEC. In a COPEC publication in 1925, he had written that 'it is God's will that every human soul should have the greatest opportunity for its fullest development'; this he said was the 'Christian motive for social reconstruction' in the areas of work, homes, education and peace, the 'fourfold challenge of to-day.' Faced with an outdated school in his parish, Cecil therefore proposed in 1935 that the school should be completely rebuilt on the same site. But these were difficult years, when funding for such projects was hard to find, and the project was shelved. Perhaps it was as well that it was, for the old school was destroyed by a flying

Donald Potter's low-relief of 'Christ and the Children' on the rebuilt parochial school, 1957.
Photo by James Funnell

bomb during the war. From then until 1957, classes were held in nearby Orchard school.

For many years before the Second World War, the 'dual system' of church and local authority schools had been seen to be unsustainable in the longer term; the war provided the impetus to deal with the matter. The 1944 Education Act put church schools and other voluntary schools in a new legal category, that of 'aided' schools. The local education authority would pay staff and running expenses, while in return for providing the site and the buildings, the church would manage the school and encourage a Christian ethos there. This new system encouraged greater consistency in the standards of voluntary and state-run schools, though it also shifted much of the responsibility for the voluntary schools to the local education authority.

The post-war rebuilding was completed in 1957, to a design by Cachemaille-Day.[124] As well as an assembly hall, it provided six light and airy classrooms each big enough to hold 40 children, which was then considered if anything a relatively small class. The Christian connection was physically marked by the installation over the main entrance of a fine and large stone low-relief of 'Christ with the Children' by Donald Potter. The connection was also marked by taking the children to the church for services, which under Miss Budd in the 1960s took place weekly on Wednesdays.

The children were not always as meekly compliant as some people today like to imagine; in 1934, the church school had to pay the large sum of £11.15.9 to repair fences and windows that they had damaged, and even as far back as 1904, the inspector noted that 'some lads allowed to use the [infants' school] room at night have much damaged the school apparatus.'[125] Nor were the children alone in their misbehaviour. An anonymous letter signed by 'A Ratepayer' in 1908 informed the authorities that 'the schoolkeeper's wife at the Percy Road School, Well Street, Hackney, is a recognised prostitute, which will be proved if enquiries are made about the neighbourhood or even in the local public houses where she calls and drinks whiskey dressed only as these women of her class do.'[126] Unfortunately, we do not know how the Rector and head teacher responded to what their correspondent alleged was 'a burning question around the school'.

The Charities

By the end of the nineteenth century it was clear to the Government's Commissioners of Charities that a thorough revision of the parochial charities was needed. After four years of deliberation, a new scheme, or constitution, setting up the new South Hackney Parochial Charities was sealed in November 1900.[127] One aspect of this revision was that all the funds except those supporting the Norris almshouse were formally amalgamated, but with a stipulation that four-ninths of the total income was to be used to assist needy young people to obtain apprenticeships, a distant echo of Sir Thomas Vyner's seventeenth century charity. Most of the remainder was to be used for the relief of hardship and for the maintenance of the almshouses and the payment of pensions to their inhabitants. This change merely formalised what was already the practice so it excited no objections.

Two other changes were controversial, however. First, instead of the trustees being the Rector and Churchwardens, a body of eleven trustees was set up, including these men – for they were then always men – together with representatives of the Hackney Vestry, the local authority, and a number of co-opted trustees. People rarely welcome the dilution of powers they have been accustomed to exercise. Rector Dodd nevertheless recognised that change was unavoidable; with apparent exasperation, he wrote 'It is no manner of use to complain about this change; it is demanded by the spirit of the times, and must be accepted and made the best of.'

The second controversial revision laid down that the area within which the trustees could make grants was the ecclesiastical parish of South Hackney. This reversed the Commissioners' 1867 decision. They may have been right about the composition of the trustee body, but they certainly slipped up here. In 1900, the ecclesiastical parish of South Hackney was but a small proportion of the parish that had been set up under the same name in 1824 and which had inherited a quarter of the ancient parish's charitable endowments. It was plainly unjust that the process of parish sub-division that went on between 1824 and 1900 should have deprived many people living in the area of the 1824 parish of access to the parochial charities' funds. Rector Dodd was not willing to accept this injustice. While the revision was under discussion, he and the other trustees agreed to appoint a parish nurse to be paid out of the charitable funds, and in announcing the appointment in the parish magazine, he pointedly wrote, 'It should be mentioned that the services of the Nurse are available throughout the whole area covered by the Charities, i.e. the original parish of South Hackney.' But the revision went through all the same, and South Hackney Parochial Charities ceased to assist many of the most needy people living in the area of the 1824 parish. The Christ Church magazine noted in January 1902 that 'There are no longer, as heretofore, gifts of Coals or any other gifts from the South Hackney Charities, but we have been enabled, by the kindness of a lady in our congregation who gave us £2 for the purpose, to supply the more needy cases.'

At around the same time, the Charity Commission gave responsibility for the property from which the income had been divided between the Hackney, West Hackney and South Hackney charities to a new body, the St John Hackney Joint Estates Charities. Its trustees were to be appointed by the constituent charities. Most of the property administered by the new body lay in South Hackney, between Well Street market and Cassland Road, and much of it had been leased under long building leases which were not due to expire for several decades.

The reconstituted South Hackney Parochial Charities continued to employ a nurse to help those who found it difficult to afford medical care. The Trustees set up a special Ladies Committee to support and supervise the nurse; one of the Deaconesses was usually a member. Grants were made

The new Norris House, designed by Alec Livock and completed in 1969.
It was given a new pitched roof in the 1990s and refurbished 2001–02
Photograph by Geoff Blyth RIBA FRSA
Courtesy of Geoff Blyth

towards such costly but necessary items as artificial teeth and eyes, convalescence, massage and simple nourishment for the sick. On the education side, the Trustees made the usual grants towards schooling, apprenticeship costs and tools, but they also occasionally assisted people who wanted to emigrate to Canada to find a better life than South Hackney offered them.

The Trustees continued to manage the Monger almshouses. South Hackney was entitled to a quarter share in the income from the joint estate, which amounted to £200 in 1938. The Blenheim Cottages, by now called 1 to 7 Church Crescent, standing on the site of the wooden cottages that Joanna Martin had given to the charity in 1670, brought in a ground rent of £80, and a deposit with the Charity Commissioners paid £161 interest. Of the roughly £450 income in 1938, £80 went in pension payments to the residents of the almshouses, and a further £125 was spent on property expenses, which included the exceptional cost of replacing the gas lighting in the almshouses with electric lighting.[128] Pensions were still paid to the almsmen, but gradually as state pensions were introduced after 1908, these were restricted and finally ceased.

A Parish in Perspective

If Rector Isherwood's impact on the church building and churchyard was something that came to be regretted, he made up for it as an active chairman of the charities. Wartime bombing had caused only slight damage to Monger House, but the century-old building was showing its age by the 1950's. However, little was done until 1964, when the back of the 1848 building was demolished and what amounted to a continuous back extension was built to provide modern kitchens and bathrooms for each of the six flats; the bedrooms and living rooms remained much as they were. Most of the money for this work came from the Borough Council as a loan, permission for which had to be obtained from a Government department that had to be persuaded that the proposed improvements were not unreasonably costly.

Norris House meanwhile continued to be managed separately by its own trustees, whose endowment was not equal to their responsibilities. The Blitz had closed the almshouse and repairs had to be delayed for ten years until 1950, when Colonel Norris formally reopened it. Members of the recently restarted Toc H branch based in Punch House, the old rectory, restored the surrounding garden as one of their 'jobs'. The facilities provided for the almswomen were however little improved upon what they had been a century earlier, and it was clear to Rector Isherwood that something needed to be done about this. But the Norris trust could not afford to make improvements, and the parochial charities' scheme did not allow any help to be given to the sister charity. In any case, as well as having suffered serious bomb damage, the Norris almshouses occupied only a small part of a large site and provided accommodation for only four residents; it was clearly a candidate for demolition and replacement, if a way could be found to finance it.

The solution was first to merge the Norris trust into the parochial charities, which was done in 1966. The trustees of the enlarged charities immediately gave their attention to the rebuilding project, Alec Livock acting as their architect. Once again a loan was made by the local authority, as a condition of which the requirement that residents be Anglicans was dropped. The new building employed a few building gimmicks of the 1960s, including a flat roof, but happily avoided the pitfalls of system building and cladding. Two aspects of the design were quickly shown to have been ill-advised: the suggestion that the windows should be double-glazed was rejected as too costly, and four of the twelve flats were bed-sits, intended for single people. The new residents moved in in 1969, under the care of resident warden Grace Powell. It is characteristic of the time that no official tears were shed over the complete destruction of the original Norris House.

The Ladies Committee did not survive long into the century, but it seems that no woman was appointed as a trustee until 1953, when Rector Parsons' wife joined the board. Several of the trustees during the 1960s and 70s were the incumbents of neighbouring parishes – which was a little odd, since it was well understood that the charities could not lawfully give assistance to anyone living outside South Hackney parish as it as been in 1900. The rector continued to chair the trustees until Rector Hickley made way for Arthur Baker in 1976, evidence perhaps of a new willingness among Anglican clergy to share leadership with the laity.[129]

Heading for a Dead End

In the 1960s, the Church of England was haunted by a sense that perhaps it was not relevant to the concerns of people at large, that it had nothing to say to them; it was certainly true that many outsiders saw it that way. Bishop Robinson's 1963 book recognised that something was fundamentally wrong. No doubt people still had the spiritual and social needs they had always had, but everyone, church people included, was living in a world that had been drastically altered by science, by technology, by the experience of war, by social change, by politics and by economics. Unless the church addressed itself to people where these changes had left them, then of course it was not going to be listened to, and of course congregations would fall away. This was a hard message for church people who themselves found real comfort in services and teaching that tried as best could be to maintain unchanged traditions that reached back to before 1914.

Church people who responded positively to the challenge generally did so in two ways, both of which were exemplified in South Hackney in the ministry of Gualter de Mello. De Mello was a young, newly-ordained Brazilian who came to South Hackney in 1964 as curate to Rector Isherwood. He lived at the Toc H house next to the new rectory and was partly paid by Toc H. One element of his approach was to try to update some of the church's services. For example, he organised a Pageant to illustrate the church's year, and arranged a special service of contemporary worship with music provided by The Mountaineers, the Church Army's Rhythm Group. But 'relevance' of this kind was essentially a veneer laid over a church that had not fundamentally changed. So the second element of his response was an attempt to reach out beyond the church-going community. He founded and led a junior and a senior youth club, which attracted, as he intended, non-church-goers, who generally resisted attempts to get them to church.

The interior of St John of Jerusalem church in the mid-1960s. The choir stalls have been moved into the crossing but there is as yet no nave altar. The marble pulpit was a temporary replacement for the original wooden one. Many women still felt awkward attending church without wearing a hat.
Photograph by a Toc H Mark III resident
Courtesy Gualter de Mello

De Mello's efforts were not enthusiastically supported either by his Rector or by many of the congregation. After little more than a year, he withdrew from the parochial ministry, becoming warden of the Toc H house, which had been rebuilt as Prideaux House[130] in 1962. Working in Hackney over the succeeding four decades, and earning Membership of the Order of the British Empire along the way, de Mello developed a Christian ministry whose cen-

Around 1900 to the 1970s: Lean Years 127

tral public expression was the provision of opportunities for people to meet, value and serve each other rather than the holding of religious services. The question that was not positively answered in South Hackney was whether these complementary elements of ministry could have been successfully combined to produce something that was both respectful of tradition and relevant to a changing situation.

A key development in South Hackney during the 1960s was a further change in the ethnic make-up of the population as increasing numbers of people from the Caribbean settled in Hackney. Race and immigration were not new issues; people had long been coming from other countries to live in Hackney, and the arrival of large numbers of Jews in South Hackney in the 1930s has already been remarked on. But they had mostly been pink; the new immigrants were brown, and this seemed to make a difference. As early as 1950, the South Hackney church magazine had tackled the 'Colour Question', which had been raised in connection with the arrival in London of many African students. Addressing a readership he assumed to be all-pink, Rector Parsons saw clearly enough the principles involved: 'What can we do? 1. Regard any colour prejudice as unintelligent and degrading. ... 3. If coloured visitors come to church then make them extra welcome. ... Coloured folk are friends, not inferior or curiosities. Like us they have faults and failings. After all the best way to treat anyone is Christ's – the way of the Golden Rule (S Matt. 7,12).'

It was sound advice, but putting it into practice proved too much of a challenge to some people at St John of Jerusalem. Many of the immigrants were Christians who had been brought up within the Anglican tradition; some of them naturally wanted to continue going to church when they came to South Hackney in the mid 1960s. It is astonishing that any church people, watching their congregations dwindle and adhering to religious teachings which explicitly stated the equality of all human beings, could fail to make the newcomers welcome. But some did. Even the rector suggested to one Caribbean newcomer that she would be 'happier' at a different church, and among some other pink church-goers there was a similar undercurrent of hostility. No doubt unfamiliarity had something to do with such reactions, but basically it was racism. It would be wrong to think that South Hackney was unusual; racial hostility in churches in Britain was so common that intending immigrants were sometimes warned of it by their clergy before leaving the Caribbean. It would also be wrong to think that all the pink members of the congregation were racist; the openness of some of them is still remembered with affection by some who arrived from the Caribbean in those years.

Attitudes in general began to improve in the 1970s as the population of the parish became increasingly multi-ethnic. The change was reflected in the St John of Jerusalem congregation – which was fortunate for the church, since without the support of the newcomers there is little doubt that it could not have survived.

Race was not the only area of social change that members of the St John of Jerusalem congregation found difficult to handle. The 1960s and '70s was a time when many of the church's traditional teachings about sex were being questioned, not only by non-church-goers, and not only in theory. The rights and wrongs of what people did that was inconsistent with church teaching is not the issue; what is very much the issue is whether the way matters were handled by the church community was supportive of people living through difficult and uncomfortable times in their lives. For example, a church-going unmarried mother was prevented from joining a Mother's Union zealous for its principal object, to 'uphold the sanctity of marriage', and a long-serving member of the congregation was forced to leave the church over an affair. Such incidents became widely known and gave the impression that the church was not for ordinary folk; many people steered clear of the church who might otherwise have belonged to its wider community.

By the early 1970s many local people assumed that St John of Jerusalem had already been permanently closed. Indeed, the sheer size of the building, and the cost of running it, falling as it did upon a small and relatively poor congregation, made some church members wonder whether closure might not be the best solution. Plans were drawn up to demolish the church and replace it with social housing and a 'worship space'. It was the dead who saved the building from the demolition ball: the cost of moving the remains of over five thousand bodies from the graveyard and re-interring them elsewhere made the scheme uneconomic. Failing that, various ideas for drastic and often unsympathetic internal sub-division were canvassed; perhaps a floor could be inserted between the nave arcade and clerestory, or a wall be built to seal off the nave from the crossing. The only obstacle to such a plan would have been its cost. When the architect Goodhart-Rendell had been consulted in 1932, he had observed that 'St John's Church, which I know well, has a certain amount of historic, but no architectural, interest'; it was merely a 'decayed Early Victorian [church].'[131] Even forty years later, the notion that the building might be valuable as 'heritage' barely surfaced. It seemed to be only a matter of time before the church was abandoned.

Chapter IV

Since the 1970s: South Hackney Revitalised

Valuing the Past

No identifiable moment marks South Hackney's emergence from the gloom that had characterised the middle decades of the twentieth century. But certainly during the last thirty years of the century, in South Hackney as elsewhere, life seemed to regain a new and vastly different normality after decades distorted by conflict and its social and cultural aftermath. Once again, developments at St John of Jerusalem church reflected the wider trends.

Despite the building of council housing schemes like Banbury, Kingshold, Parkside and Frampton Park estates on bombed areas, the melancholy evidence of war was all around in 1970. Corrugated iron fences round bomb sites and wartime emergency prefabricated homes were still to be seen, as were derelict buildings awaiting redevelopment. The corrugated iron did not finally disappear until the 1990s, when the last large derelict area in the parish was redeveloped as housing. This was the area near the church around the Albion pub and Hampden Chapel, which the local authority proposed in 1985 to use as a site for travellers. The proposal was unpopular and a number of public meetings organised by both the Council and local residents took place in the only building in the area large enough to accommodate the hundreds of people who wished to attend: St John of Jerusalem church. There was a sense that local people were reclaiming the local parish church as well as asserting their right to call the local authority to heel.

The opponents of the travellers site were able to cite the fact that the area around the church, with its mid-nineteenth century buildings, had been declared a Conservation Area, with the church itself being 'listed' along with

Monger House. This was evidence of the growing awareness of 'heritage', the idea that old and familiar buildings were important to local people irrespective of whether they were of historic or architectural interest. It was enough that their presence over many years spoke of continuity in a world in which so much was changing so quickly. As one of the oldest surviving buildings in the area, South Hackney parish church naturally benefited from this new realisation. In the early 1990s, the Government's conservation agency, English Heritage, funded essential work on the crossing and the aisles, as well as the replacement of sandstone facings which had weathered badly.

Nor was it only official bodies that took a new view of the church; taking their lead from Rector Evan Jones's concern for beauty and propriety in worship, the congregation shared in the re-evaluation. The desire to beautify the church and to take pride in its history re-emerged. A massive crucifix was obtained by Rector Jones from the disused church of St Augustine Haggerston, to which it had been given by parishioners in memory of their much-loved vicar, Father Wilson. Hung from the chancel arch, the crucifix instantly made architectural sense – though it would certainly have scandalised the church's architect. The carved woodwork was restored by Charlie Payne, who had come to South Hackney from the West Indies. A sculpture in memory of Nell Hudson was given in 1984 to adorn the steps of the font, and stained glass windows were commissioned in memory of the committed church work given by Arthur and Dorothy Baker during the lean years. And of course the book you are reading is itself a product of this change of view.

A Wider Family

The social developments that had proved such a stumbling block in the 1960s continued, but they too were seen in a new and more positive light. The arrival of two groups of newcomers gave the parish the raw materials for revival, reversing the trend towards non-church-going social homogeneity. From around 1970, increasing numbers of people from the West Indies came to the church and found a real welcome. Feeling themselves to be very much newcomers and often intending eventually to return to the West Indies – as indeed a few eventually did – some of them for many years felt it inappropriate to participate in long-term decisions about the future of the church. As years passed, however, those who had come from the West Indies became key members of the church community. Among the earliest Caribbean people to become stalwart members of the congregation were Eddie and

Poster for the autumn bazaar, 1972. The tradition of parish bazaars was established in the late nineteenth century as other sources of funding dried up. The annual pre-Christmas bazaar continued to be an important source of revenue past the end of the following century. Courtesy of the Rector

Since the 1970s: South Hackney Revitalised

Rosalind Thomas from Dominica. Eddie eventually became Churchwarden, and among his successors was Barbadian-born Waple Kellman.

A new wave of newcomers, this time from West Africa, began to join the St John of Jerusalem congregation from about 1985. Among the first African families was the Paul-Worikas from Nigeria; Datoru Paul-Worika became Churchwarden in 1998. Newcomers came not only from the Commonwealth, but also from other European countries. It became commonplace to hear languages other than English being spoken over coffee after Sunday morning service. Gradually, the clear distinction between pink and brown church-goers began to fade as children were born to parents whose ancestors had come from different parts of the world.

Newcomers were not always from overseas. The proximity of South Hackney to the City, its relatively low property prices and attractive open spaces, and the new esteem enjoyed by Victorian and Edwardian buildings tempted increasing numbers of middle class professional people to buy homes in the parish, especially after about 1990. 'Gentrification', as this process was called, had its down side – the children of local people were priced out of the market for homes near their parents – but it brought in money which helped tackle the old shabbiness of the area, and it added another element to the stimulating mix of people to be found in South Hackney and in its parish church.

In the years after 1970 or so, church-goers had to come to terms with the fact that practically every social norm of sexual behaviour was altering in ways that challenged the church's traditional teaching about such matters. The divorce rate soared to nearly four times the level that had caused the church such concern in 1946. Contraception became freely available. Increasingly, couples lived together and had children without getting married. Homosexuality became better known, not least because of the AIDS/HIV issue, which had a theological dimension that had to be addressed. The people of St John of Jerusalem gave up any attempt to shy away from these issues. In particular, divorced and homosexual people were welcomed into the church community along with people whose lives had followed a different pattern; what was sought and offered was a sense of fellowship in dealing with life's joys and challenges in a way that was informed by the gospel.

Rector Hickley and his wife, Terry, came to South Hackney in 1970. Because they had a young family, they almost without trying made people with children feel more at home in the church. As a result, all aspects of church life were revitalised: the choir was re-populated with children and church rambles were once again popular. It took more effort to ensure that this welcome spread as far as those whose family life was unconventional or unfortunate, an effort that was informed by Terry's work as a marriage guidance counsellor.

As far as HIV/AIDS was concerned, Rector Jones set the tone when he welcomed a homeless, non-church-going person with AIDS to come to live at the Rectory. He and a parishioner, Elizabeth Taylor, were among those who in 1989 founded the Christians in Hackney AIDS Initiative, which attempted to help Christians develop an approach to AIDS/HIV that did not welcome the virus as a divine punishment for sexual impurity.

The absorption into the church community of people with widely different backgrounds and experiences proved enriching. There was the obvious fact that without them the church would have ceased to be viable, either financially or as a community. But just as significant was the opportunity it offered for everyone to learn from and about each other. A 2001 exhibition entitled The Harvest of the Nations invited members of the congregation to display items that reminded them of their home countries, which included, as well as the UK, Barbados, Brazil, Germany, Ghana, India, Jamaica, Korea, Nigeria, Sierra Leone, and USA. Social events such as bring-and-share Sunday lunches and Burns Nights helped to mould this wonderfully various congregation into a cohesive whole, and also enabled everyone to become more closely acquainted with the many different traditions represented in the congregation.

Church Affairs

The pattern of services changed again during this period. Only one Sunday service was held, a morning Eucharist; baptisms were often incorporated in this service, which would have pleased the first Rector. The register of services shows that attendances rose steadily: an average of 27 communicants in 1971 doubled to 59 in 2001, while Easter communicants rose from 40 to over 100 in the same years. Although the 1990s was designated by the Church of England as the Decade of Evangelism, this rise probably had more to do with the change in local demography than with conventional evangelism. But evangelism takes many forms, and perhaps it is right to understand the opening of the congregation towards those who were not regular church-goers as one of them.

Just as it had been in the 1850s, the Holy Week and Easter period was the focus of the church's year, but the services had changed greatly even since the

1950's. The changes were characterised by the substitution of liturgical drama for the lectures and sermons of earlier years. Palm Sunday was marked by the congregation processing to and around the church holding aloft their palm crosses. On Maundy Thursday evening, after the commemoration of the events of the Last Supper, the church was stripped of its ornaments while a psalm was recited in the growing darkness. The main Good Friday service involved the singing of the Reproaches and of the Passion Gospel. In connection with the lighting of the Easter Fire on Easter Eve, some variety was introduced, with the traditional series of vigil readings alternating with innovations including dramatic monologues and a sequence of readings and music for Easter. Some of these services, like the Christmas carol service and special evensongs, offered the opportunity for people who were not regular church-goers to take an active part in services. At least some of them found this a valuable opportunity for them to revisit or explore for the first time the possibilities of religious observance.

While attendance at regular services rose, the use made of the church for rites of passage continued to fall. For example, in 1961, there were 107 baptisms; the figures for 1981 and 2001 were 36 and 21 respectively. As the church's continued resistance to divorce encountered the need of couples somehow to solemnise re-marriages, there was an increase in the number of blessings of civil marriages performed in the church.

These were the years when the Church of England practically abandoned the old Book of Common Prayer. As elsewhere new forms of service were introduced at St John of Jerusalem for the Sunday Eucharist. Rector Hickley introduced the use of the chasuble and other eucharistic vestments. The new services and the use of vestments symbolised the growing closeness of the Anglican and Roman Catholic churches in the 1970s and '80s. Another example in South Hackney was the pilgrimage to the Holy Land made jointly by clergy and people from St John of Jerusalem and St John the Baptist Catholic church in 1987. The involvement of the St John of Jerusalem clergy in the work of St Joseph's Hospice grew deeper in these years, with the result that funds were made available for St John of Jerusalem to have an extra member of staff. Although some of the lay staff at the Hospice stumbled at first over the unfamiliarity of dealing with non-Catholic priests – and especially with Terry Hickley as a priest's wife – the clergy of St John of Jerusalem found their spiritual ministry welcomed enthusiastically by the Sisters and clergy at the Hospice as well as by the medical and nursing staff.

The pace of Anglican-Catholic ecumenism in South Hackney slackened in the 1990s, partly for local reasons but also partly because of the Church of

England's decision to ordain women as priests. Thanks to the presence of All Saints House a century before, South Hackney parish had had an earlier experience of the formal ministry of women than most other parishes. It was therefore fitting that during her ministry at St John of Jerusalem, Patricia Farquhar progressed from being a deaconess to being one of the first women priests in England. She was also appointed a Prebendary of St Paul's, the first member of the St John of Jerusalem staff to hold such an appointment since Henry Handley Norris.

Among the notable events of these years was one of the last sermons preached by Trevor Huddleston. The venerable old man who had been thrown out of South Africa for his opposition to apartheid before becoming Bishop of Stepney preached from a chair to a rapt congregation, recalling his visit to South Africa as the guest of the triumphant Nelson Mandela. Huddleston would undoubtedly have applauded the fact that among his successors as bishop in east London was Uganda-born John Sentamu, whose visits to the church included those to open the refurbished Monger House and to dedicate the Baker memorial windows.

Despite the generous help of the diocese and of English Heritage in maintaining their magnificent church building, the congregation still needed to hold fund-raising events both to cover day-to-day expenses and to make a contribution to diocesan funds. The century-old tradition of jumble sales continued, at once a recycling scheme, an opportunity for bargains and a means of raising funds. The Christmas Bazaar with its grand prize draw was a regular feature and a key element in fund-raising. In holding such events where the free benches used to stand in the nave of the church, not only was a medieval attitude to the church building revived, but people who might not otherwise do so came to be familiar with the interior of the building whose exterior was such a presence in the area.

Looking Outward

During the lean years, the church in South Hackney, as elsewhere, had tended to see survival and the maintenance of an unchanging tradition as almost its only tasks. As the experience of those years bore witness, this was a strategy that could lead only to oblivion. From the 1970s, it became increasingly obvious that the church needed to engage with a changing world, seeking to discover what the gospel might have to say to people who were outside its ambit, and who might never attend its services. So as well as drawing a

AN UNEXPECTED CAREER: THE REV PREBENDARY PATRICIA ANN FARQUHAR

One of the Church of England's first women priests, preparing for retirement, looks back on her career.

I grew up in Tottenham, quite near the Spurs' White Hart Lane ground. A friend and I attended the local Anglican church together and we were confirmed when we were 13. I was a Brownie and Girl Guide and eventually became the Guider for two Brownie packs. I went to the local state primary and secondary schools. I knew I wanted to work with people so on leaving school I trained as a therapy radiographer. I was working at the North Middlesex Hospital, treating people with cancer, and still living in Tottenham when I felt the call to full-time ministry in the church. I had been very involved in the life of two churches in Tottenham and was greatly encouraged in my vocation by the curate of one of the churches. My parish priest was rather less enthusiastic about the idea of a woman being anything other than a parish worker! In those days – this was 1976 – women were not allowed to be ordained in the Church of England, and there was no prospect of that changing. So although I was sent by the Bishop of Edmonton to train with male ordinands at Lincoln Theological College, I thought that I was going to spend my career as a deaconess.

When I'd finished at Lincoln and was due to return to take up a post in Edmonton, there was no suitable post available, as often happens. So I crossed the river to St Paul's in Deptford where I spent two years. Although I loved the area and people, it was not an easy time for me. It was an Anglo-Catholic church, and my role was limited to what the men would allow me to do. I preached occasionally, but I wasn't invited to read the Gospel or take part in processions, and I had no formal seat in church. The Head Deaconess of London realised how difficult things were for me and suggested a move to St John of Jerusalem, South Hackney. I accepted, but not out of desperation; what made it feel so right was the connection with St Joseph's Hospice, where I felt my previous experience as a therapy radiographer would be useful.

I arrived in South Hackney in 1980. Here the atmosphere was quite different. There was no difficulty in being seen as a woman in ministry. I was delighted to discover that the East London Deaconess House had been located in South Hackney and that there was a commemorative plaque in St John's! But Evan Jones had been Rector for only been a couple of years, and before him the parish had had a married rector whose wife had been willing to play the role of the traditional clergy wife. At first some of the congregation were confused about my role, and expected me to be a kind of paid vicar's wife. I had to be quite firm at first as I explained that I was the equivalent of a curate, not a vicar's wife! For five years or so, I worked in the parish full time, concentrating particularly on work with the elderly and youngsters and at the Hospice.

The Reverend Prebendary Patricia Farquhar in her stall in St Paul's Cathedral, 1997.
Photograph by Geoff Taylor

Then, when I began to think I might move on, the Bishop of Stepney appointed me Dean of Women's Ministry. I enjoyed this work; it involved supporting and giving pastoral care to women in ministry in Hackney, Islington and Tower Hamlets. I also represented the women at the bishop's staff meetings, which I felt was a great privilege and responsibility. At the same time I continued to do as much work in the parish as I could manage. The debate in the Church of England about women's ministry hotted up in the 1980s, and in 1987 the decision was taken to ordain women as deacons. The ordination service for seventy-one women deacons in St Paul's Cathedral on 22 March 1987 was wonderful!

The Head Deaconess for London retired at this time and responsibility for the selection of women candidates was delegated to each episcopal area. So I was appointed assistant Director for Ordinands for Stepney Area, with responsibility for encouraging vocations and supporting women through the selection and training process. In 1992 I took over as Director of Ordinands for both men and women, a post I held until 1998.

When Evan Jones left the parish in 1992, the difficult position of women in ministry was really brought home to me. As well as my work with ordinands I was still doing the parish pastoral work and trying to hold the congregation together, yet every week for almost a year I had to find a male priest for the Eucharist on Sundays. Women were finally allowed to become Church of England priests in 1994. This was great, wonderful – something I had never expected to happen. My ordination in St Paul's and my first celebration of the Eucharist in April 1994 were both wonderful occasions. But the ordination of women also proved to be painful for me. Although the theological debate combined with the experience of women as deacons had convinced some people who had been doubtful about it – including Evan – some close friends in ministry were deeply opposed to the ordination of women. Some of them left the Church of England and became Roman Catholic priests, while others stayed in but under a cloud. A bit of me felt responsible for their unhappiness. On the other hand, quite a few of the Roman Catholic friends and colleagues I had met though my work at the Hospice were very supportive.

My appointment as a Prebendary of St Paul's Cathedral in January 1997 came as a totally unexpected honour. As a member of the cathedral team, with my own stall in the choir there, I attend the great services, like the millennium service for England and the celebration of the Queen Mother's 100th birthday in the year 2000. But there's important work to be done there: I am part of the pastoral team and I'm very conscious that I'm there to represent the ordinary people of South Hackney, especially when I preach in the cathedral. And of course, as only the second woman to be appointed as a prebendary, I'm still conscious of that special responsibility too.

My work for successive bishops has meant that I have stayed in South Hackney for twenty years, much longer than I'd intended, and

> longer, I'm told, than any previous clergy-person here apart from the first two rectors, back in the nineteenth century. Being in one parish for a long time has its advantages; you get to know people very well and see them change as you change. I've baptised the children of people I baptised when I was new here, and it has been a privilege to journey with people through the last years of their lives. When eventually I leave, I shall take with me happy memories of South Hackney, and a feeling of contentment. I suppose that I feel the main part of my ministry in South Hackney has been to encourage other people to grow and develop and to achieve their potential – which I suppose is only right given the way my own ministry has grown from very small beginnings thanks to the support and encouragement of many people along the way.
>
> Patricia Farquhar retired to Norfolk in 2001. Her successor as assistant priest was Patty Bailey, a primary school teacher who served South Hackney part-time in a voluntary capacity.

broader range of people into the church, the St John of Jerusalem church community reached out during these years to meet non-church-goers on their own terms. During the 1980s, this was to some extent accidentally facilitated by political developments in Hackney. Control of the local Council's almost traditional Labour majority was taken by people whose unwillingness or inability to effectively manage the Borough's affairs combined with their political principles earned them the popular sobriquet 'the loony left'. The situation was one in which the efforts of voluntary organisations, including in South Hackney the church as well as Gualter de Mello at Prideaux House and the opposition to the travellers site, took on a new significance.

Sometimes outreach was a matter of church-going individuals becoming deeply involved in community activities of one kind or another. So, for example, Mavis Bucchan visited Holloway Prison every week as a volunteer for many years, not to thrust Christianity down anyone's throat but simply to help the women prisoners with their children. Waple Kellman was appointed as a lay chaplain to Homerton Hospital, while a lay reader, Neil Hughes, became a local Councillor in the 1990s. Churchwarden June Pipe served as Chair of the Governors at Homerton College of Technology.

In other cases the church was able to give more direct support. We have seen how the church in South Hackney had tried to tackle the problem of alcohol abuse in earlier years. The problem had not gone away in the late twentieth century, but the approach was now neither censure backed with threats nor preventive indoctrination. The idea behind Alcoholics Anonymous was that those who had striven to control their abuse of alcohol were best placed to encourage and support others who faced the same struggle, having their own resolve strengthened in return. By its nature as a self-help group, AA required little of the church other than accommodation, but the church was pleased to be able to help in this small way. The church was able to offer similar help to a Wakirike community group from Nigeria.

In 2000, the church building was the setting for the display of sixty panels of the Millennium Tapestry, created by school children throughout Britain to celebrate diversity, history and hope. The magnificent display was visited by local schools and left the church feeling almost undressed when it was dismantled. Another children's initiative that the church supported with accommodation was the Rucksack music scheme, enabling young children to begin their musical education.

Bell ringers – like organists – often have a complicated relationship with the church. The magnificent peal of eight bells at St John of Jerusalem is one of the best in north-east London, and in 1979 a team of ringers was once again formed to practise the ancient English art of change-ringing. Some people complained about this, seeing it as a form of noise pollution, but probably many more appreciated this touch of almost rural calm in inner-city South Hackney, and at least one person from the Caribbean was drawn by the ringing of the bells to become in due course a stalwart member of the congregation.

The awareness that church life could not go on in a vacuum led in the mid-80s to an effort to find out what the general public in the area thought about life in South Hackney and about religious matters. Church members interviewed at random almost two hundred people living in different types of housing in the parish. The results, while not surprising, do give some unvalidated confirmation to common assumptions. Most people admitting any religious adherence still said 'Church of England', but about half the sample disclaimed any religious membership. As for what people found most important in their lives, God came a poor third to family and health-and-happiness.

Almost twice as many interviewees had a broadly positive view of the Christian churches in the area as were prepared to tell interviewers that the church was 'daft' or irrelevant. Despite large numbers valuing the open spaces and general friendliness of South Hackney, life there was said to be blighted by shabbiness and crime – problems that the Council was expected to do more to tackle.

Music Plays its Part Once Again

Music was a significant element in the revitalisation of St John of Jerusalem church, which turned out to be a fine setting for both concerts and recordings. Here the destruction of the 1960s brought an unexpected benefit: the removal of most of the chancel furniture had created a large, unimpeded stage. Moreover the apse about which people had complained when the church was built proved to have a warm acoustic and a vault that helpfully projected sound into the nave.

When the newly formed Hackney Singers – itself part of the transformation of Hackney in the 1980s – was looking for a venue for its first public concerts, one of its members arranged for the choir to use her parish church in South Hackney, and it has continued to hold its Christmas concert there ever since.

In 1993 James Funnell left the Hackney team ministry to become Rector of South Hackney, and his interest in the arts became an asset to St John of Jerusalem church. His own enthusiasm for and expertise in music led to the formation of a second Hackney choral society, the St John of Jerusalem Festival Chorus, which performed in the church under his direction with the support of an orchestra drawn from his family's musical circle. Their first production, Handel's *Messiah*, was given in the church in 1997 as part of the world-wide BT Voices for Hospices event, the collection naturally going to St Joseph's Hospice. It was followed by other works from the standard choral repertoire. These concerts created a momentum that allowed concerts of more esoteric music to be successfully presented in the church.

Still more ambitiously, on Palm Sunday in 2000 the Festival Chorus and its Chamber Orchestra were joined by soloists and the choirs of two local primary schools in singing Bach's *St Matthew Passion*. A member of the orchestra wrote later, 'I still remember that weekend with something of a sense of wonder … It was truly amazing to find an event so well run, such a part of the local community and, ultimately, so moving.' This remarkable

WHO GOES THERE?

A survey of users of the St John of Jerusalem church building in 2002 elicited a wide range of replies. Here is a thought-provoking selection.

What if anything does Christianity mean to you?

- A faith I have always known.
- Spiritual growth and support.
- Believe in God and live by his laws.
- Habit, a sense of ritual, part of my upbringing.
- Perhaps it is more about 'doing' than 'being' – a way of controlling the masses.
- Lost my faith gradually in early adulthood, but I respect believers and enjoy taking part in music and services.
- I believe wholeheartedly in God.
- The way to righteousness and godliness.
- Sharing my faith with others.
- That Christ died for us to save us from our sins.
- That there is 'that of God' in everything and everyone.
- It is absolutely fundamental to my life.
- We had chapel daily at school – hence 'antibodies'.
- Hope; compassion; being accepted.
- I believe strongly in spiritual forces, spiritual awareness and intelligence; however, religion of any kind does not appeal to me.
- Service, love and care in the community.
- The word of God keeps everyone in the family straight.
- Atheist since schooldays; some cultural attachments and sharing of some Christian values.
- It is part of my everyday life.
- Stability; familiarity; hypocrisy – very mixed feelings I'm afraid.
- I am a committed Christian, a Bible-believer.
- The peace of ritual. I'm a sort of Christian agnostic these days.

- Friendliness and helpfulness of the clergy and congregation.
- Hearing the bells.
- The routine of worship each Sunday.
- Exhibition of school banners 2001.
- Christmas performance by the school.
- Performance of the St Matthew Passion – an incredibly moving and memorable event.
- Seeing my children confirmed, and now my grandchildren.
- [Z's] funeral.
- The intoxicating music of Bach and Handel.
- The cold!
- The people.
- Meals with the whole church.
- Hard seats.
- Development of friendships and new relationships.

What if anything about the building is particularly significant to you?

- The spire because it's so visible.
- Its hugeness!
- The sanctuary windows.
- It reminds me of the church in my home town.
- The broad aisle.
- The soaring view from the west door.
- The green spire, as it was one of the first words my daughter said.
- The fact it can host all types of events for the community.
- Its height.
- The new stained glass window which incorporates a picture of my godson.
- The timber of the pews and the quality of the light.
- The view of the spire from the surrounding area.
- Good acoustic.
- The front entrance.
- It's just a beautiful building.

- Not sure – still working on that one! My relationship with God is a real part of my life and ever changing like most relationships.
- Believing in God and staying a good person.
- Not much.
- Belief that there is a higher deity who guards and cares for me, even if I go wrong or find some things quite inexplicable.
- It has always been the basis of my life and has served me throughout; my belief in God is profound and total.

What or who has caused you to keep in contact with St John's?

- I have enjoyed the services and concerts and made some good friends.
- Friends and fellow-worshippers.
- Warm and friendly clergy.
- Level of support I received in difficult times.
- Friendship and music.
- A wish to actively participate in the community.
- Services.
- I really appreciate the chance to sing in a good choir with a good-natured, optimistic conductor.
- The people I know there.
- Apart from the worship itself, much kindness, friendliness and support in times of joy and sadness.

What significant memories do you have of the church?

- Being confirmed by Bishop John.
- Getting married there.
- Being welcomed by Mrs [X] on our first visit.
- The fascinating sub-culture of bell ringing.
- [Y's] memorial service.
- Seeing the door open and the lights on on Sept 11, 2001.
- Being blessed for our wedding.
- Art exhibitions by local people.
- None yet!

event was destined to hold a special place in the memory of all who were present either as participants or as listeners, and a compact disc recording of the performance was released to help them recapture the atmosphere of the moment. As the CD booklet noted, the performance was as 'authentic' as any could be, for 'here was a performance being given in a church, during Holy Week, in the vernacular, without an admission charge. ... Just as authentically but more astonishingly, the performers, though of course familiar with the work, had not sung or played it before, at least not in the roles they took this time.'

Such concerts helped to give the parish church back to the people of the area, including those who were not church-goers, some of whom surprised themselves by speaking of 'our church'. The concerts also symbolised a realisation that the church's contribution to the enrichment of people's inward life was not merely or always a matter of getting them to attend church services. This was the real answer to the question to which we saw Rector Dodd giving a pat answer in 1890s, and with which Rector Parsons was struggling in the 1950s.

The Parochial Charities

South Hackney Parochial Charities continued to run its two almshouses on a shoestring until the sale by the St John Hackney Joint Estates Charities of most of its controlled-rented residential estate off Well Street in the 1980s. The proceeds were handed over to the parochial charities for investment, the income from which enabled Arthur Baker's successor as chairman, Geoff Taylor, to carry through a major refurbishment of both almshouses, once again bringing them up to current standards.

Like so much of the architectural legacy of the 1960s, the rebuilt Norris House had not aged gracefully. Architect Geoff Blyth's refurbishment plan provided the elderly residents with showers rather than baths, double glazing, and a lift, while a new pitched roof gave a level of watertightness that the original flat roof had quickly lost. Four of the eleven flats were specially adapted for people with physical disabilities and the garden was redesigned with residents of limited mobility in mind, making it easy to sit out in attractive surroundings.

The refurbishment of Monger House presented a different set of problems. The nineteenth century building had provided six dwellings which, even with the 1960s extension, were far too small. The refurbishment therefore reduced

The Bishop of Stepney, Dr John Sentamu, plants a tree to mark the refurbishment of Monger's almshouse, 1997
Photograph by Geoff Taylor

the number to four. Since it was a listed building, consent for improvements had to be obtained from English Heritage. While the trustees were at one with English Heritage in wanting to retain George Wales's 1848 facade, they were unhappy with the requirement to keep alive the memory of the building by retaining space-consuming features such as disused and unseen chimney breasts whose chimneys had disappeared in the 1960s. Interestingly, some of the joists from the original 1669 almshouse which Wales had been authorised to reuse were again reused. In a further change, a paid non-resident warden, Patrick McDermott, was appointed to support all the almshouse residents.

The new wealth also enabled the parochial charities to be pro-active in encouraging organisations to apply for grants to enable them to help local people help themselves or to help deal with the results of deprivation. A number of parenting programmes were set up under this initiative, while several schools benefited from large grants for equipment and environmental improvements. In keeping with the general thrust of seeing how the best traditions of the past might be rejuvenated for the new millennium, the parochial charities obtained the agreement of the Charity Commission to a revision of their governing scheme taking account of the social changes of the twentieth century and enabling the charities to offer assistance throughout the original South Hackney parish. A century-old injustice was thus put right.

Seeking to better discharge its financial responsibilities to the parochial charities, the St John Hackney Joint Estates Charities began to make other changes that affected the local environment. A hard-to-let factory block in Well Street was converted into offices for small businesses and named 'Celia Fiennes House' after the social investigator who lived nearby in the early eighteenth century. More ambitiously, steps were taken to profit from the steep rise in local property prices to bring new life and new residents to the charities' blocks on the east side of Well Street market, which had long been in decline. The Trustees were keen to maintain the involvement of the church charities in the community's built environment, realising, in the words of their chairman, that they were part of the 'institutional heritage' of South Hackney.

The Church School

If there was a similar renaissance of the church school in the closing years of the twentieth century, it had to do more with national trends in education than with local initiative. During the early 1970s, the school was once again struggling to find enough staff, and the head teacher, the fascinating and complex Leon Chandler, was reduced to making desperate appeals for anyone who could teach. This naturally distracted attention from raising standards; teachers were largely allowed to get on with the job as they saw fit. Inspections by the Inner London Education Authority were informal and private affairs compared with those conducted in the 1990s; reports were not published and parents had only anecdotal evidence about the comparative performance of local schools. Even in a church school, the responsibilities of the managers, including their *ex officio* chairman, the Rector, were circumscribed.

The story of how these things were changed by nationally imposed curricula, rigorous testing and inspection, and more delegation of management control is not part of this history. But the effect of the changes is. Fortunately, as the Government delegated more and more responsibility to the governors, Rector Funnell was appointed, bringing with him not only his own experience as a teacher in Hackney, but also insights provided by his wife Jean, a local primary school teacher.

One important aspect of the changes was the introduction of the regular testing of pupils and the publication of the results, which both stimulated and measured improvement. The measured performance of St John of Jerusalem School in English, maths and science improved markedly in line with that of other Hackney schools. But there is more to education than such measurable results, and the 2002 inspection by the Office for Standards in Education (Ofsted) identified as the particular strengths of the school its music teaching, ethos of care, provision for the one tenth of pupils with special educational needs, and provision for moral, social and cultural education. It is perhaps noteworthy that the report was astonishingly detailed compared with those written a century before, when inspectors were equally concerned about standards but did not have word-processors at their disposal.

In contrast to the situation in the early part of the twentieth century, by the 1990s schools run by churches and other religious bodies had come to be perceived by both Government and the public as being able to provide a better education than schools run by the local authority. Their results were generally among the best, but there was debate as to whether or not there was something in the ethos of religious schools that produced the good results. It might have been merely that these schools were attended by children whose parents were prepared to make the effort needed to secure a place in one of them, and that with such enthusiasm for education behind them the children would probably have done well in almost any school. One incidental result was that parents who thought that a place in St John of Jerusalem school could be secured by attendance at the church occasionally appeared at services for a few months. In fact about half of the school's pupils had no connection with any Anglican church. Faithful to its founder's intention, the school did not see its role as serving the sectional needs of Anglican families but rather as offering to children of the parish generally an education informed by Christian values.

Even before the revolution in education administration, the school premises had begun to be expanded and improved. A separate nursery block was built in 1985, partly with help from the Sir John Cass Foundation. The bleak tarmac of the playground was immeasurably cheered up by the creation of garden areas. The blowing-down of the 1960s point blocks that had towered over the school, and their replacement with two- and three-storey homes returned to the school the sense of scale it had had when it was built.

At the Turn of Another Century

As the first two hundred years of the St John of Jerusalem community drew to a close, it faced a new challenge. Whether or not it turns out that the world really changed on 11 September 2001, when terrorists killed thousands of people in USA, there certainly seemed to be a new readiness to face issues that had previously been overlooked. Church-goers were faced with significant choices: were they first and foremost members of the Christian church, radically distinct both from those who claimed no religious affiliation and from Muslims and members of other religions? Or were they called to see in everyone of all faiths and none people whose fellowship they could accept and celebrate in their common pilgrimage through life, while still acknowledging their own indebtedness to the Christian tradition and the teaching of Jesus? Some indication of the response of the congregation of St John of Jerusalem may be gathered from their spontaneous applause for the imam of the Kingsland Road mosque when he addressed them during the Sunday service a few weeks after the terrorist attacks on USA. Such a response was perhaps to be expected from a community that had already learned to share their building and fellowship with the Jews, Hindus, Quakers, Humanists, avowed atheists, agnostics, lapsed Christians and others who belonged to the Festival Chorus. It was ironic that this wide sympathy should be found in a church whose dedication recalled the appalling events of the Crusades, and whose builder was so narrow in his outlook.

Nothing was likely to change the ebbing and flowing of trends that the previous two hundred years had witnessed. The broadmindedness of eighteenth century figures like Elizabeth Cass and Jeremiah Marlowe has returned in the last forty years or so after a long period when the church generally and in South Hackney in particular had been characterised mostly by a narrow outlook. The sense of history that Norris had exemplified but which was forgotten in the mid-twentieth century has come back in the form of the heritage movement. The unfortunate homogenisation of the area during the seventy years after about 1895 was sandwiched between periods when it profited from the presence of a diverse population. The best that could reasonably be hoped

WHAT FUTURE FOR SOUTH HACKNEY CHURCH?

Rector James Funnell introduces proposals to the Parochial Church Council, June 1995

Before I came to South Hackney as Rector two years ago, one of the major factors I had to consider before deciding to come to this parish was the church building. It is a huge building as well as a striking one. Through its size, its beauty, its style of architecture and the detail of its decoration, it was meant to have an impact on the local community. I think it can reasonably be said to have been at the heart of the community in 1848 when it was completed and first used for public worship. It was undoubtedly the largest and most important building here whose purpose was indeed the worship of God. But I believe it was more than that because it was the focus and inspiration of many community activities in South Hackney. Some of these activities may have happened in the church, but if they did not happen in the church itself, I feel sure that it was the church community which met in the church building which generated the purpose and energy for them to happen.

The second point about the church is that it was built to seat a thousand people. The pews needed to be rented to secure a good seat for oneself and one's family. The wide middle aisle was full of free seats, and the gallery, where the remains of the old pipe organ now are, was used to provide extra seating. The church was new and therefore would not have needed much maintenance and any that was required could have been managed by the giving of its reasonably prosperous congregation. Perhaps it is worth noting that two other large churches were built in the neighbourhood later in the nineteenth century, St Augustine, Victoria Park and Christ Church, Gore Road. Fortunately we do not still have the problem of deciding what to do with them because they were both demolished after the second world war and their parishes, or parts of them, were incorporated in ours.

It hardly needs saying that the situation has changed greatly since 1850. We now have a regular worshipping congregation of less than a hundred. In the context of east London Anglican churches that is not particularly small, but our church was built for a much larger congregation. Our present needs do not require a building anything like the size of St John of Jerusalem. It would be much easier for us if we had a completely different kind of building. The size the structure, the complexity of its design and decoration and its age mean that the present building has become a major problem for us.

In coming to this parish I had to make a decision. Did I want to take on a parish where a considerable amount of time and energy would be needed to deal with the building, which I knew would take me away from other aspects of being a priest which in many ways I consider to be more important?

But I did decide to come to St John of Jerusalem, for three main reasons.

First, I decided that the building need not, indeed should not, be considered only as a problem. It could be considered as a real asset and advantage if it could be viewed positively and if some changes and developments could be made.

Second, I considered that it was important to try to return this important building to its original status as a focus for the whole community, not only as a centre for the worship of God but as a possible centre for wider community use.

Finally, I considered that to do this was to be involved in the essential mission and purpose of the church, reaching out in love to those among whom we as a church are set, and responding to Christ's call to show the love of God to our neighbours.

It was for this reason that I suggested to the church council that we set up a small group to think about how this building could be developed, and it is members of this Building Development Group who are to continue this presentation to you. We hope to underline for you the beauty of the building and those aspects of it we consider it is essential to retain. We want to point out its deficiencies and the facilities which we think a building which we hope can be used more widely must have. Finally we want to share with you some possible ways of achieving the improvements which we think are now essential to returning this fine old building to its place in the centre of our community.

The reordering at the west end proposed by Mark Julian in 2002. The plan includes a community space, meeting room, offices, kitchen and toilets – and a lift to the rooms in the lower tower.
Photograph of architect's model, by James Funnell
Courtesy of the Rector and Mark Julian

> The proposals put to the church council after Rector Funnell's introduction were drawn up by church architect Tom Hornsby, taking careful account of the requirements of English Heritage as well as of the concerns identified by the building development group. A few years later a more modernistic plan by Mark Julian was put forward. The main features of both plans included the building of a suitable partition across the church, creating spaces for community activities at the west end of the church, with a kitchen and toilets at the west ends of the aisles. The font was to be moved back towards the centre of the nave. The later plan included a meeting room in the tower, accessed by a lift, and a fully-equipped crèche in the north transept. The idea of developing the church building to make it more suitable for community activities was broadly welcomed by the church council and later by the congregation. But it was expensive, estimated to cost over a third of a million pounds if carried out in its entirety. The idea is still on the table; so is a range of ideas about how the facilities to be created could be used by and for the wider South Hackney community. All that is missing is the money.

was that further change would be bearably gradual and would take account of at least some of the lessons of history.

Nor were the constants to which this history has borne witness likely to come to an end. They include human frailty and erring judgement, the inspiring role of music, the dangers of alcohol and other drugs, the power of creativity and imagination, the difficulty of finding an adequate outward expression for individual spirituality, the challenge of deprivation in all its forms, the movement of people into and out of South Hackney, and – what is perhaps the most reassuring, come what may – the sheer attractiveness and interest of most people most of the time.

Envoi

A Shade Returns

For almost a quarter of its history, the church and parish of St John of Jerusalem, South Hackney, found itself under the powerful leadership of the remarkable first Rector, a man of boundless energy and firm views. It is tempting to wonder what Henry Handley Norris would make of his parish and its church if it were possible for him to revisit South Hackney today.

He would not be in the least shocked to discover that the rural hamlets of his childhood have become heavily built-up areas. He recognised that the encroachment of buildings onto fields and gardens that had already begun by the time of his death would continue unstoppably, and the church he built was planned with this development in mind. What might however surprise him is that he would find that the boundaries of the park and gardens round his own mansion are still marked, by Victoria Park Road, Lammas Road, Church Crescent and the back garden fences of Groombridge Road. He might also be surprised to see that the Lammas lands of which he was a part-owner have not been built over but retain their old shape and are still called Well Street Common; even the ancient east-west path across the common is still there.

He would certainly be pleased to recognise reminders of his family in the names of several streets built on what had been his estate. His son and heir Henry Norris had moved away from Hackney to near Banbury and named one of the streets after that town. Catherine Norris's Kentish family connections are remembered in the names of Penshurst, Edenbridge, Southborough and Groombridge Roads. Oddly, there never was a Norris Road, but the first Rector would no doubt enjoy discovering himself recalled in the name of Handley Road. And in Handley Road he would be struck by the sight of the crest he claimed as his own – the stag's head with its neck pierced by an arrow – etched into a window of the almshouse which, he would happily discover, had been built in his memory and named after him: Norris House.

The interior of St John of Jerusalem church in 1985. There is much that would disturb the first Rector. It is odd that almost all depictions of the interior are from the north side of the nave
Courtesy of Carol Halliday

The other almshouse, Monger's, he would instantly recognise as the one over whose erection he had quarrelled with George Wales, though he might regret the disappearance of its massive chimneys and leaded windows. By contrast the building on the site of the school he knew would be entirely new to him, and its educational objectives and methods would be no less unfamiliar than the building.

Norris would no doubt take a certain grim satisfaction in the disappearance of several of the local non-conformist establishments that had riled him in his days as Rector, but perhaps any irritation he might feel at finding Hampden Chapel still in use would be moderated by relief at the continued existence of 'his' church. He could hardly guess at the vicissitudes it has survived. The copper spire would irritate his gothic purism; he would probably fail to make the connection between the disappearance of the original spire and the relatively poor quality of the stone he had been able to afford for the enormous church.

Approaching the building through a churchyard whose apparent lack of graves would puzzle him, he might be gratified by the sound of a choir rehearsing inside, continuing the tradition of music making he had fostered. He would however be shocked to discover that the singers, though under the baton of his successor as rector, included people of many different religious affiliations and none. The state of the church's interior would certainly offend him: where, he would ask, is all the decoration, stained glass and furnishing that had cost him so much fundraising effort? The uncompromising presence of the crucifix in the chancel arch would appal him as a blasphemously Catholic intrusion. And he might tut-tut about the faintheartedness of his successors who had failed to vault the crossing in stone.

But what would radically disorient him would be attendance at a typical Sunday service in the church. The Book of Common Prayer by which he set such store has been abandoned. A woman, and, worse, a woman in a chasuble, celebrates the Eucharist. What's more she stands facing not Godward but towards the relatively small and very mixed congregation of only around ninety people, at an altar set up in the crossing. If he stayed for the sermon, he would note many differences from the sermons he published, in length, in tone, in teaching, in assumptions. Norris, the great defender of the power and authority of Anglicanism against Rome, non-conformity and secularism, could be forgiven for reflecting bitterly that little of it remained but its shell.

He would certainly be resistant to the idea that the institution he had so zealously defended was itself a shell around something precious and intangible that continues to lie at the heart of what St John of Jerusalem church seeks to be in the twenty-first century. It remains for many a symbol of the state of flourishing and fulfilment each of us is invited to aspire to, and the wonderfully various people who use it and the buildings associated with it in their different ways accept that invitation and offer their friendship to those whose paths cross here.

Appendices

Appendix 1: Rectors of South Hackney

1831	Henry Handley Norris, MA Cambridge, Prebendary of St Paul's and Canon of Llandaff *perpetual curate from 1808*
1851	George Palmer Lockwood, MA Cambridge *curate from 1845*
1871	Ridley Daniel-Tyssen, MA Oxford
1885	John Henry Lester, MA Cambridge, Canon of Lichfield
1890	Vivian Rodwell Lennard, MA Cambridge
1897	Joseph Arthur Dodd, MA Cambridge
1911	Kenneth Durnford Iliff, MA Oxford
1914	Basil Staunton Batty, OBE, MA Cambridge, FRAS
1918	George Thomas McLean, MA Dublin
1928	Francis Fitzgerald-Doherty, MA Royal University of Ireland, FRGSI
1930	Henry Cecil, AKC
1937	Montague Richard Parsons, MA Durham, BD MTh London
1956	James Isherwood
1970	Peter Michael Hickley
1978	Evan Hopkins Jones
1993	Norman Richard James Funnell, BA Lampeter

Appendix 2: Vicars of Christ Church, Gore Road

1869	John Cruice Egan, MA MD Glasgow, MRIA, FRCS of Ireland *curate at St John's, 1863–69*
1890	Francis Robert Walker, AKC *curate at St John's, 1883–90*
1898	Thomas Ward Chambers, MA Cambridge *curate at St John's, 1894–98*
1908	Carrick Ransome Deakin, MA Oxford
1923	Lambert Francis Eyre Foxell, AKC, Honorary Chaplain to the Forces, Prebendary of St Paul's
1954	*Parish amalgamated with St John of Jerusalem, South Hackney*

Appendix 3: Money before Decimals: £sd

Before decimal currency was finally introduced in Britain, an ancient and awkward system was used. The pound was divided into 20 shillings, each of which contained 12 pence, and large sums were expressed in terms of whole pounds, whole shillings and pence, for example, £12.12.6. For smaller amounts, shillings were indicated by 's', sometimes elongated to '/'; 'd' (for the Latin *denarii*) indicated pence. As an added complication, 21 shillings or £1.1.0 was referred to as a 'guinea'. Those who never used this system would be appalled by how complicated it made calculations! In 1971, when the pound was divided into 100 new pence, the shilling of 12d became 5p; £12.12.6 thus became £12.62½ in decimals. The ½p later fell into disuse. Since translating the face value of sums in £.s.d currency into decimals gives no idea of the real value at the time, they are best left in the form originally used.

Principal Sources

Exhaustive reference footnotes would be out-of-place in a book such as this, and I hope readers will forgive me for keeping them to a minimum. For any who find that difficult, let me say that the principal sources, apart from general and church histories and interviews, are to be found by searching under the name of the church or parish in Hackney Archives, London Metropolitan Archives, Lambeth Palace Library, Guildhall Library and the National Monuments Record. Books by various clergy and the architect are mostly in the British Library. I have tried to make it possible for anyone who wishes to do so to retrace my steps through the sources by signposting them in the text. Generally, where a source is not given, it is a church magazine in one of the collections I have used; the year will, I hope, be clear, and the location can be identified from the list below.

BOOKS, MAPS AND ARTICLES

In Whole or in Part About South Hackney

Ashpitel, W	*Plan of the Parish of St John-at-Hackney*	1831 reptd 1985
Batchelder, D	*From Tower to Tower Block*	1979
Booth, C	*Life and Labour of the People in London* Third Series	1902, 1903
Brabner, C	*Directory of Hackney*	1872
Bumpus, TF	*London Churches Ancient and Modern*, Second Series	1908
Clarke, B	*Glimpses of Ancient Hackney and Stoke Newington*	1894 reptd 1986
Makerson, C	*Guide to the Churches of London*	1889
Mander, D	*Strength in the Tower*	1998
Pevsner, N	*The Buildings of England: London II* (rev. Cherry, B 1998)	1952
Walford, E	*Old London*	1884 reptd 1989

| Watson, I | Gentlemen in the Building Line | 1989 |
| Watson, I | Hackney and Stoke Newington Past (2nd ed) | 1998 |

By or About People Connected with South Hackney

Novello (pub)	Twelve Hymns with Tunes	1897
Cecil, H (ed)	The Fourfold Challenge of Today	1925
Cecil, H et al (eds)	Brightest England and the Way In	About 1920
Doherty, F	Sunshine in Religion	1911
Ferrar, WJ	Sacred Poems	1903
Foxell, LFE	King Charles I, who saved the Church	1950
Hakewill, EC	The Temple	1851
Hakewill, R	Treatise on the Hakewill Family	unpublished
Lennard, VR	Woman: Her Power, Influence and Mission	1910
Mayhew, H	'The Seller of the Penny Short-Hand Cards' in London Labour and the London Poor	1851
Norris, Hugh	A Little History of the Norris Family	unpublished
HH Norris	See separate list below	
Smith, RJ	'Letters from a Hackney Curate, 1828' in Hackney History vol. 2	1996
Southgate, W	That's the Way it Was	1982

Books and Other Publications by H H Norris

Norris, HH	Substance of a Speech Delivered at the Anniversary Meeting of the Auxiliary Bible Society	1814
Norris, HH	A Manual for the Parish Priest	1815
Norris, HH	A Letter to the Rt Rev the Bishop of London	1818
Norris, HH	A Letter to Lord Liverpool	1822
Norris, HH	The Origin, Progress and Existing Circumstances of the London Society for the Propagation of Christianity among the Jews	1825
Norris, HH	A Scriptural Investigation of the Doctrine of Holy Places	1829
Norris, HH	An Admonition to Members of the Church of England	1835
Norris, HH	Marriage Scripturally Considered	1837
Norris, HH	The Good Shepherd	1839
Norris, HH	Ritual Conformity	1842
Norris, HH	A Pastor's Legacy	1851

PERIODICALS CONTAINING MATERIAL ABOUT SOUTH HACKNEY

Illustrated London News: 1845 and 1848
The Builder: 1848, 1871 and 1957
The English Churchman: 1850
The Ringing World: 1981

COLLECTIONS CONSULTED

Hackney Archives Department (HAD)	Amherst Papers Norris Papers Tyssen Papers Church Magazines, C20 Routh Letters Publications by H H Norris Census returns Various illustrations
London Metropolitan Archives (LMA)	Papers and publications deposited by the Rector of South Hackney Charity Commissioners Reports, 1818–1837: Middlesex
Lambeth Palace Library (LPL)	Papers of the Bishops of London Incorporated Church Building Society papers
National Monument Record (NMR)	Various illustrations
Royal College of Organists	Bumpus collection of church anthems Various compositions by John E West
Collection of Dr Melvyn Brooks, Karkur, Israel	*A History of the Parochial Charities of Hackney and Stoke Newington*, 1856 South Hackney parish magazines, 1888 Christ Church, Gore Road, magazines, 1902 *A History of Mare Street Baptist Church*, 1947 Various illustrations
Collection of Francis Erridge	Material about Arthur Erridge
Guildhall Library	Papers deposited by the Diocese of London, under 'St John of Jerusalem, South Hackney' and 'Christ Church, Gore Road'

Principal Sources

STANDARD REFERENCE WORKS

Crockford's Clerical Directory
Dictionary of National Biography
Venn's *Alumni of the University of Cambridge*
T A Walker *Admissions to Peterhouse ... Cambridge*, 1912
Victoria History of the Counties of England: Middlesex, volume 10 – Hackney

WEBSITES

www.johnwest.org.uk – John West, organist
www.knights-of-st-john.co.uk – The Order of Knights of St John of Jerusalem
www.smom-za.org/bgt/ophthhosp.htm – St John's Ophthalmic Hospital, Jerusalem
www.hkbu.edu.hk/~johnny/sjo.htm – the Order of St John
www.newadvent.org/cathen/07477a.htm – Hospitallers of St John of Jerusalem
www.sewanee.edu/All_Saints/ – Erridge's windows at the University of the South
www.dfes.gov.uk/performancetables – school performance tables, 1996–2001
www.ofsted.gov.uk/inspect/index.htm – school inspection report, 2002

INDIVIDUALS

Batchelder, Sian and David	Jones, Rev Evan
Bucchan, Mavis	Kellman, Waple
Byrd, Jean and John	Lineker, Roger
Claydon, Graham	Lloyd, Lily
de Mello, Rev Gualter R	Miller, G (chairman of J Wippell & Co. Ltd)
Drakes, Doris	
Fyson, John	Parsons, Dr Richard
Gray, Ron	Powell, Grace
Henderson, Russell	Rankin, Lily
Hickley, Rev Michael and Terry	Sorrell, Robin
Hiza, Joan (nee Hudson)	Thomas, Eddie
Jakeman, Stephen	Visick, George

OTHER SOURCES

Memorials in the church
Gravestones in the church graveyard
Peal boards in the church's ringing chamber

Notes

1. Ashpitel's Map 1831 and Brooks & Saint *The Victorian Church: Architecture and Society* 1995, p4
2. Charity Commissioners' Reports for Middlesex 1818–1831, p367 ff
3. LPL: Porteous 10 f 148
4. The plan and front elevation are in LPL at Porteous 10 ff 146 and 147.
5. LPL: Porteous 10 f150
6. Clarke 1894, p173; a watercolour of the building in 1830 is in the HAD. (Plate 1)
7. HAD: D/F/TYS/24
8. Clarke 1894, p230
9. HAD: D/F/TYS/24
10. Quoted in G Best *Temporal Pillars* 1964 p 258
11. 'Surriensis' A response to H H Norris's *An Admonition to Members of the Church of England on Neutrality* 1835 p 17
12. LMA: P79/JNJ/350
13. Letter from J O Routh of Homerton Cottage to his son at Christ's College Cambridge, 30 March 1835. HAD: MA 1360
14. LMA: P79/JNJ/350/4
15. R J Smith 'Letters from a Hackney Curate, 1828' in *Hackney History* vol 2, 1996
16. LPL: Howley 10 ff 102–103. The census has the teacher's name as Williamson.
17. LMA: Charity Commissioners' Reports for Middlesex, 1818–1837, p 373
18. LMA: P79/JNJ/248: Dec 1885
19. HAD: M3422
20. LMA: P79/JNJ/237
21. Clarke 1894, p 135
22. *Ritual Conformity*, in HAD
23. E C Hakewill *The Temple: An Essay* 1851 p119
24. LMA: P79/JNJ/1 – 2
25. HAD: D/F/NOR/8/1
26. *loc cit.*
27. *loc cit.*
28. *The Builder* 1848, p 137

29. *The Builder* 1848, p 355
30. *The Builder* 1848, p 388
31. Bumpus 1908, p 157
32. This paragraph is based on LMA: P79/JNJ/350/9 and HAD: D/F/TYS/16
33. LMA: P79/JNJ/1/20
34. LMA: P79/JNJ/268
35. HAD: D/F/TYS/16
36. The commoners had rights over Common land all year round. Their rights over Lammas land lasted only between August and March; for the rest of the year the land owner used the land for his crops.
37. LMA: P79/JNJ/248
38. LPL: Tait 440/91 and 441/384
39. LMA: P79/JNJ/268/4/4
40. LMA: P79/JNJ/288, LMA: P79/JNJ/279/5, LMA: P79/JNJ/196/2
41. LMA: P79/JNJ/279/5
42. In the collection of Dr Melvyn Brooks.
43. LPL: Blomfield 51 ff 24 and 71, 51 f 30, 51 ff 142 and 143, 53 f 214
44. LPL: Tait 122 ff 308 – 309, ff 217 – 221
45. Gore Road then emerged into Victoria Park Road opposite Fremont Street.
46. *The Builder*, 1871 p 555 and LPL: ICBS papers, f 7002
47. LMA: P79/JNJ/207 and Guildhall Library
48. LMA: P79/JNJ/209
49. The admission charge on the third day was reduced for the benefit of less well off parishioners.
50. HAD: D/F/AMH/448
51. LMA: P79/JNJ/218, 221, 222 and 223
52. LMA: P79/JNJ/ 228 and 229
53. Harrington lived at 20 Penshurst Road with his wife, two children and a maid-servant.
54. HAD: *East London Church Chronicle* March 1893
55. Southgate 1982 p39
56. *op. cit.* pp 11 and 24
57. *op. cit.* p 40
58. *op. cit.* p 39
59. *loc. cit.*
60. Southgate 1982 p 59
61. *op. cit.* p 41
62. *op. cit.* pp 26–27
63. *op. cit.* p 39
64. *op. cit.* p 59
65. *Life and Labour of the People in London* Third Series: *Religious Influences: London North of the Thames, Outer Ring* 1902 pp 92 and 89

66. The plans are in Guildhall Library.
67. Booth, loc. cit.
68. Unless otherwise noted, the information comes from church magazines in the LMA or the Brooks collection.
69. LPL: Tait 440/91 and 441/384
70. In the LMA
71. Brabner's Borough of Hackney Directory, 1872 (Hackney central library)
72. In the church magazine for March 1898, the sacristan asks for a set of red stoles; he makes no mention of other vestments.
73. In his *Woman: Her Power, Influence and Mission* 1910, page 197
74. LMA: P79/JNJ/236/4
75. See C Mackerson *Guide to the Churches of London* 1889. The undated specification in LMA: P79/JNJ/215 appears to describe this organ.
76. Church magazine, March 1888
77. Private communication from Roger Lineker, who comments that Elliott's organ music was 'very much of its time.'
78. Annual statistical returns in the church magazines
79. J Grierson *The Deaconess* 1981 p 28
80. Census for 'Church House', 1901
81. Church magazine, February 1895
82. Booth, *op. cit*, p 81
83. Booth, *op. cit*, p 80
84. Booth, *op. cit*, p 102
85. Church magazine, January 1901
86. LPL: Creighton 1 f 64
87. Booth *Life and Labour of the People in London* Third Series: *Religious Influences: Summary* 1903 p 418
88. Church magazine, July 1895
89. Census, 1881, 1891, and 1901
90. I have not been able to track down a copy of Lockwood's book, referred to in his Venn *Alumni* entry.
91. LMA: P79/JNJ/248
92. LMA: P79/JNJ/99/1
93. Church magazine, April 1896
94. LMA: P79/JNJ/ 236/1
95. Christ Church magazine, January 1902
96. LPL: Creighton 1 f 64
97. LMA: P79/JNJ/324/2
98. *History of the Parochial Charities of Hackney and Stoke Newington* 1856; Brooks collection
99. Victoria County History: Middlesex vol. 10: 'Charities'
100. He lived at 9 Cassland Road with other clergy of the parish.

101. LMA: P79/JNJ/270 and 267
102. LMA: P79/JNJ/267
103. *ibid.*
104. LPL: Jackson 2 ff 402 and 403 and Creighton 1 f 65
105. The dean seems not to have acknowledged that doubting is not something you can do confident of where it will bring you, nor something you can decide not to do.
106. Victoria History of the County of Middlesex: Parish of Hackney, p 123
107. LPL: Creighton 1 f 64
108. LPL: ICBS f 12088
109. LMA: P79/JNJ/201/5
110. See the LCC map of bomb damage, in LMA
111. Foxell 1950 pp 7 and 11
112. Cecil *et al.* n.d. (c. 1920) p v
113. *op. cit.* p 29
114. LMA: P79/JNJ/212
115. LMA: P79/JNJ/66
116. LMA: P79/JNJ/
117. LMA: P79/JNJ/216
118. LMA: P79/JNJ/583
119. LMA: P79/JNJ/238
120. LMA: P79/JNJ/328/7
121. LMA: P79/JNJ/324/5 and 328/21
122. LMA: P79/JNJ/328/12
123. LMA: P79/JNJ/324/5
124. *The Builder* 1957, p 586
125. LMA: P79/JNJ/324/2
126. LMA: P79/JNJ/328/3
127. In the South Hackney Parochial Charities archives
128. LMA: P79/JNJ/260
129. Much of the information in the above four paragraphs comes from the SHPC Minutes for 1951–83, held in the charities' archives.
130. The original Prideaux House was replaced by a row of houses in 2002.
131. LPL: ICBS f 12088

Index

Africa 134, 135, 137, 142
Agnes, the Lady 6, 117
alcohol 48, 62, 64, 78–9, 81, 93, 142, 155
All Saints House 10–11, 75, 79, 104, 137
almshouses
   buildings 39f, 50, 125, 147–8
   funding 40, 49, 124
   residents 48, 93–4
   warden 125, 148
Amherst – see 'Tyssen'
architects and architecture 8, 26f, 29, 31f, 34f, 38, 39, 50, 54, 111, 121, 125, 129, 147, 155
   see also 'Hakewill, E C'
Arnold, Rev Thomas, author 46
Ashworth, Susan, stained glass artist 119, pl5

Bailey, Rev Patty, curate 141
Baker, Arthur, churchwarden pl4, 119, 126, 132, 137, 147
Banbury, estate 107, 131
Band of Hope 62, 79
Bannister, Mother Alice pl3, 75
baptism 25, 66, 67, 135, 136
Bartholomew, Major 76
Batty, Rev B S, Rector 101, 161
beadle 22–3
bells, bellringing 29, 32, 37, 99–100, 111, 142
Bennett, Mr, organist 109

Blomfield, Bishop C J 17, 32, 50, 52
Blyth, Geoff, architect 147
Book of Common Prayer 24, 66, 119, 136, 159
Booth, Charles, social investigator 64, 76, 77, 78, 80
Bowdler, Rev Mr 37
Boys' Brigade, The 62, 76
British and Foreign Bible Society 13, 15
Bucchan, Mavis, prison volunteer 141
Budd, Miss, headteacher 122

Cachemaille-Day, N F, architect 111, 121
cars 67
Cass, Dame Elizabeth 19, 151
Cass, Sir John Cass Charity 11, 19, 97, 150
Cecil, Rev Henry, Rector 97, 98, 102, 103, 104, 106–7, 120
Chandler, Leon, headteacher 149
Chang, family grave 58
charities, parochial 4, 19, 20–1, 88f, 93–4, 122f, 147f
Charity Commissioners 89, 93, 122–3, 149
choir, church 56, 66, 68–70, 71, 73, 109
Christ Church, Gore Road 53, 54, 61, 62, 63, 64, 75, 79, 81, 95, 96, 97, 105, 108, 116, 123, 152, 162
Christchurch Square 54

Index 171

Christmas 4, 23, 70, 74, 78, 79, 133, 136, 137, 143, 145
church attendance 2, 25, 54, 60, 64, 66–7, 97, 108, 135f
Church Building Society 25, 28, 54, 103
Church Commissioners 21, 80
Church Lads Brigade 76, 100, 101, 104, 108
church rate 85
church services 24, 60, 64f, 135f
Clapham Sect 9, 16
Clarke, Dr Benjamin, Hackney memoirist 8, 22
class, social 8, 17, 18, 21, 47, 59, 61f, 64, 78, 86, 97, 106, 134
Cockshutt, John, almsman 93
communion 4, 19, 23, 24, 50, 60, 64, 66, 67, 70, 104, 159
confirmation 67, 74
COPEC 120
Cornell family 101
Crawford, family grave 58
Crieff (Scotland) 84
Croix de Rozon (Geneva) 7
Crucifixion, The 68, 70, 72
cultural societies, in relation to the Church 77–8, 109, 147
Currey, Henry, architect 38, 39

Daggett, John, organist 68
De Kewer, John, businessman 8, 16, 21
de Mello, Rev Gualter, curate 126, 127, 141
deaconess(es) 74–5, 102, 123, 137, 138, 139, 140
demography
  population 3, 47
  migration 5, 47, 98, 124, 132, 134, 135, 155
divorce 58, 108, 136
Dodd, Rev Joseph, Rector 56, 66, 78, 80, 88, 99, 109, 123, 147

Doherty, Rev F F, Rector 98

Easter 4, 64, 66, 67, 135, 136
Eck, Rev H, chaplain 75
ecumenism, or lack of it 14, 19, 79, 106, 107, 136
education, policies towards 3, 16, 87, 120–1, 150
Egan, Rev Dr John, curate and Vicar of Christ Church 81, 84
Elgar, Sir Edward, 71–3
Elliott, R B, organist 70
English Heritage 132, 148
Erridge, Arthur, stained glass artist 111, 112–13, pl4
Evans, C, beadle 22, 23, 59

family connections 12, 13, 18, 26, 38, 59, 81, 157
Farquhar, Rev Patricia, curate 137, 138–141
Ferrar, Rev W J, curate and poet 70, 84, 90–2
First World War – see 'Great War'
Forbes, Mr W P, parishioner 108
Foxell, Mr, entrepreneur 116
Foxell, Rev Lambert, Vicar of Christ Church 105, 116
Frampton family, local landowners 19
Frampton Park 7, 19, 47, 59, 107, 131
Freemasons x, 103
fundraising methods 16, 17, 28, 57, 78, 85–6, 133, 137
Funnell, Rev James, Rector 143, 150

Gerard, founder of St John of Jerusalem hospital 6, 117
graves, graveyard 8, 9, 58–9, 115, 125, 129, 159
Gray, Nutter, undertaker 9
Great War 75, 97, 98, 100, 102, 104, 105
green man 32

Hackney Friendly Society 21
Hackney Phalanx 9, 14, 16, 18, 24, 25
Hackney Singers 143
Hakewill, E C, architect 29, 31, 32, 50, 57, 115
Hakewill, J H, architect 54
Harrington, William, lay reader 60
harvest festival 67
Hensler, Mr 85
heritage 16, 24, 129, 132, 149, 151
Hickley, Rev P M, Rector 115, 126, 134, 136
holidays and outings 62, 75, 79, 84
Hopewell, family grave 58
Howley, Bishop W 19
Huddleston, Bishop Trevor 137
Hudson, Nell, parishioner 132
Hughes, Neil, councillor 142

Iliff, Rev K D, Rector 81
Ireland, connections with 37, 52, 81, 98
Isherwood, Rev J, Rector 108, 115, 125, 126

Jackson, John, failed almsman 93
Jews 13, 98, 109, 128, 151
Jones, Rev E H, Rector 132, 135, 139, 140

Kellman, Waple, churchwarden 134, 141
Kibbler, Dr A & Mrs 77
Kingshold, estate 100, 114, 131, 151

Lammas land 47, 157
Laprimaudaye, Rev Mr 37
Lennard, Rev V R, Rector 56, 60, 67, 70, 75, 84, 86, 94
Lent 64, 65, 66, 68
Lester, Canon John, Rector 56, 60, 67, 68
Levi, Joyce, teacher and choirmistress 109

Livock, Alec, architect 124, 125
local authorities
　Hackney Vestry 122
　Inner London Education Authority 149
　London Borough of Hackney 125, 131, 141, 143
　London County Council 116, 120
　London School Board 87–8
　Metropolitan Board of Works 89, 101
　Metropolitan Borough of Hackney 110
Lockwood, Rev G P, rector 42, 47, 50, 51, 52, 64, 65, 67, 84, 85, 88

Marlowe, Jeremiah 20, 93, 151
marriage 61, 67, 77, 129, 135
Martin, Joanna 20, 40, 124
Matthey, family grave 58
Maud, Sister 75
May, Rev J, curate 18–19, 22
McDermott, Patrick, warden 148
Messiah 72, 143
Meynell Gardens 75, 97, 104
Michell, family grave 58
Millennium tapestry 142
mission church 59, 60, 64, 77, 97, 104, 107, 114
Monger almshouse 5, 11, 19, 20, 21, 39f, 41, 50, 88, 93, 94, 107, 124, 125, 132, 137, 147, 148, 159
Mothers' Meeting 75, 77, 78, 109
Mothers' Union 104, 129
Moulins, Roger de, Grand Master of Order of St John of Jerusalem 6
music and the church 23, 68f, 109, 136, 143, 147, 155
Muslims 6, 7, 151

National Society 14, 16, 17, 37, 44, 87
Nightingale, Florence, social reformer 58, 110, 117, 129

Index 173

Noah's Ark 27
Non-conformity 4, 14, 16, 19, 30, 32, 50, 52, 80, 107, 159
Norris almshouse 49, 93–4, 108, 125, 157
Norris, Catherine Henrietta – *see* 'Powell, Catherine Henrietta'
Norris, Col H Du C, benefactor 110, 111, 125
Norris, Henry, son of Rev H H Norris and Catherine Powell 42, 50, 56
Norris, Rev H H, first Rector 9, 12–15, 16, 17, 18, 19, 21, 23, 24, 25, 27, 28, 29, 32, 39, 40, 41, 42, 44–6, 47, 48, 49, 52, 64, 80, 82, 84, 86, 87, 99, 115, 137, 151, 157, 159, pl2
Norris, William, local builder 37, 49, 89
North Street (now Northiam Street) 10–11, 61
Novello & Co 70, 71

organ(s) 22, 37, 56, 68, 110, 119
organist(s) 22–3, 68, 70, 71–3, 99, 104, 109, 112, 119, 142
outreach 60, 75, 106, 126, 135, 136, 141, 151
Oxford Movement 9, 16, 24, 41, 54

paintings 15, 116
Parker, Charles, architect 50
Parochial Church Council 101, 152
Paroissien, Rev C, curate 18, 45
Paroissien, Rev G, first Rector of West Hackney 9, 18
Parsons, Rev M R, Rector 108, 109, 126, 128, 147
pastoral work 18, 19, 71, 75, 81, 82f, 84, 92, 146
Paul-Worika, Datoru, churchwarden 134
Payne, Charlie, parishioner 132
Pevsner, N, architectural critic 28, 113
pew renting 28, 61–2, 85, 86, 102

Phillips, family grave 58
Phillips, Thomas, portraitist 15, pl2
Pipe, June, churchwarden 142
political connections 14, 24, 63, 64, 80, 107, 141, 142
Potter, Donald, sculptor 121, 122
Powell, Catherine Henrietta, wife of H H Norris 13, 17, 49, 112, 157
Powells, stained glass studio 36, 112
Powell, Grace, warden 125
Prideaux House 127, 141
Prin, Gilbert, headteacher 88
Prout, Ebenezer, editor of *Messiah* 71
psychology 12, 42, 50, 56, 85, 106
Pulley, C H, Clerk 22
purity 75, 76, 101, 135

race 128–9, 134, 137
Rawbone, Ann 22, 23, 24
Rectory, The 64, 80, 81
religious attitudes 4, 13, 61f, 64, 67, 94–6, 97, 100, 105f, 126, 136, 137, 142, 143, 144f, 151
ritual, matters relating to 24, 25, 52, 115, 136
Robinson, Bishop John 115, 126
Robinson, Thomas, businssman 56, 59
Roman Catholicism 7, 14, 25, 30, 32, 42–3, 52, 136, 159
Royal Martyr Church Union 105
Rucksack, children's musical group 142

school, parochial
   achievements 87, 116, 120, 150
   administration 88, 116, 149f
   aims and methods 17, 39, 87, 150
   buildings 10–11, 16, 37, 38, 87, 120, 121–2, 150
   funding 16, 17, 37, 87, 116, 120
Second World War 102, 104, 110, 121, 152
Secularists 94

Sentamu, Bishop John 137
Sequira, Rev E R, curate 81
sex, matters relating to 75, 79, 81, 84, 122, 129, 134, 135
Sharon Gardens 97
Society for Promoting Christian Knowledge 13, 15, 25
soup kitchens 62, 78
South African War 100
Southgate, Walter, autobiographer 61–3, 64, 76, 79
St Andrews – see 'mission church'
St Augustine of Canterbury, Victoria Park 53, 54
St John-at-Hackney, church 4, 8, 9, 12, 18, 21, 88, 89
St John of Jerusalem church building, 1810–1848 8, 10–11, 27, 28, pl1
St John of Jerusalem church building, 1848 to the present 10–11, 28, 30, 34f, 54f, 111, 129, 132, 143, 145, 154
St John of Jerusalem Festival Chorus and Orchestra 143
St John of Jerusalem, Order of 5, 6, 8, 32, 117
St Joseph's Hospice 111, 136, 138, 143
St Mary of Eton, Hackney Wick 53, 54
St Matthew Passion 143
St Michael and All Angels, London Fields 26, 39, 53
St Thomas's Hospital 37, 87, 97
Steib, R sexton 22–3
Sunday school 60, 74, 75, 79, 104, 108, 114, 116
survey 142, 144–6
Sutton House 22

Tait, Bishop A C 52
Taylor, Elizabeth 135, 143
Taylor, Geoff 147, 149
Thomas, Eddie, churchwarden 134

Toc H 103, 106, 125, 126, 127
Tossell, James, headteacher 88
travellers site, opposition to 131
Travis, family grave 59
Tyler, family grave 58
Tyssen, family, patrons of Hackney parishes 5, 9, 56, 59, 80, 84, 110
Tyssen, Rev R D, Rector 56, 59, 84

Vinall, family grave 58

Wakirike, Nigerian group 142
Wales, George, architect and builder 39–41, 89, 148, 159
Walsham How, Bishop W 60, 75, 94
war, attitudes to 76, 100, 101, 105–7
war, effects of, in South Hackney 102, 104f, 105f, 107
war memorial 98, 101, 102, 111
Watson, Joshua 14
Watson, Rev J J, Rector of Hackney 5, 12, 26
Well Street Common 47, 157
West Hackney, Parish of 8, 9, 21
West Indies 58, 128, 132, 135, 142
West, John E, organist 68–70, 71–3, 90, 104, 112
Wigginton, William, archtect 54
Williams, Charles, schoolmaster and nonconformist 17, 19, 22
Williams, Dr 52
Williams, George, almsman and alcoholic 48–9, 93
windows, stained glass 36, 108, 110–11, 112–13, 117–19, 132, 137
Winkley, Charles, churchwarden and Mayor 99, 101
women and the church 12, 17, 19, 74f, 93, 104, 109, 119, 123, 125, 137, 138f
Wood, M A, bellringer 99
working men's club 77, 104

Index 175